0

.

PRICELESS - A Successful Organizational Culture

Contents

First Edition: September 2014
ISBN Numbers:

eBook: 978-981-09-2371-6
Digitised Book: 978-981-09-2372-3
Hardback/ Hardcover: 978-981-09-2369-3
Paperback/Softcover: 978-981-09-2370-9

For permissions requests, contact:
Raj Singh and Vanpeak Pte Ltd. (Singapore)
71 Ubi Crescent, Excalibur Center, #04-11, Singapore 408571
Phone: +65 62640889
Website: www.vanpeak.com

A Successful Organizational Culture: Driven, Focused, and High-Performing

Introduction

A primary responsibility of organizational leaders – corporations, family businesses, governmental agencies, non-profit organizations, or any other type of organization – is the design and continuing development of organizational traits that provides a positive return and motivates the collective efforts of the organization's team but yet maintaining individual compensation for extraordinary contributions.   It is *organizational culture* that is the forefront element in establishing and continuing the competitive advantage and the positive performance that successful companies enjoy.

And why do many companies and organizations fail when they shouldn't? It is due to a failure in ethical concepts and practices. Organizational leaders simply do not give the attention to an organization's culture that it deserves.

Developing an organizational culture, ethos, ideas, and practices that will give your organization a competitive edge is not easy and it does not happen overnight. It is deliberate, thoughtful and planned. It takes trial, reassessment, modifying and then retrial. It is an evolution not an invention. We will be discussing several leadership strategies and tactics for creating a successful organizational culture that actively promotes organizational success rather than focusing solely upon individual success. And why do this? While successful organizations are the breeding grounds for entrepreneurs, successful organizations are able to retain a great number of their talented individuals. And very successful organizations are choosy in which of their talented individuals they retain. Yes, there are times in which organizations do not keep successful individuals.

We will be looking at three fundamental descriptors of a successful organizational culture: what drives it, on its focus, and what makes it perform. We also speak to a few particular tools and cultural elements that have proven invaluable to the developing of successful organizational cultures.

And we cannot have an organizational culture without an organization of people. Traditionally, it has been held that the most important person in a successful company is the client. However, in the past few decades we have seen companies that focus upon employee satisfaction over client satisfaction and have produced remarkable successes with this concept. Why? Well, let's take a lesson from Southwest Airlines, a perennial top ten most admired company in the world:[1]

Our Culture differs from other companies in that, in our "order of importance," we put our Employees first, then our Customers, then our Shareholders. Many companies feel you have to appease the customers or shareholders first, but Southwest Airlines has the magic formula that makes us an admired company: Happy Employees=Happy Customers=Increased Business/Profits=Happy Shareholders! We believe that, if we treat our Employees right, they will treat our Customers right, and in turn that results in increased business and profits that make everyone happy.[2]

Hence, engaging employees *in the right way* is certainly a major component of a successful organizational culture.

---

[1] "World's Most Admired Companies." Fortune. March 17, 2014. Accessed August 11, 2014. http://fortune.com/worlds-most-admired-companies.

[2] "Southwest Airlines 'Gets It' With Our Culture." Nuts About Southwest. March 22, 2011. Accessed August 11, 2014. http://www.blogsouthwest.com/southwest-airlines-"gets-it"-our-culture/.

A Successful Organizational Culture

An organizational culture can be defined as a collection of behaviors that are developed, used, and sought after by members that organizational group. Cultural behaviors are the actions and behaviors of group members based upon a set shared notions and views that are associated with a way of life. Often times these notions and views are not formally shared but communicated through "unofficial" or "informal" behavior and communiques of official and unofficial group leaders.

What this means is that an organizational culture is the result of how the majority of the members of the organization act. How the majority acts is greatly influenced by not only the official managers but also through the actions of the dominant group members who may not be in managerial roles. The mediocre, but strong-willed salesperson who has been around for ten years often has greater influence in the sales department than the more successful sales manager that has recently come onboard.

Therefore, in order to develop the successful organizational culture that you desire for your company, you will be looking at, modifying, encouraging, and discouraging certain types of behavior. We cannot get around that no matter how politically incorrect that may sound. There are successful behaviors and there unsuccessful behaviors.

Characteristics of a Successful Organizational Culture

It is no surprise that most highly successful enterprises, groups, companies, and cultures have common characteristics. There are many, but the following traits tend to be the most common ones:

- Leaders not only lead but are constantly teaching others to be leaders.

- It is recognized that not are managers are leaders.
- Key managers and leaders display a positive attitude even during difficulties.
- Everyone at all levels of the organization is very aware of the organization's policies, procedures, rules, plans, and strategic goals.
- The organization values the opinions of all group members.
- All group members believe that they are vital and important members of something that is bigger than they are.
- Organizational problems are solved through and with representative groups.
- Improvement is acknowledged continuously, but
- Improvement is never viewed as a completed task; rather it is seen as a continual business process.
- Innovation and creativity is an integral philosophy that permeates all thinking and behavior.
- Steadfast bureaucrats and administrators and professional politicians are viewed as liabilities.
- Developing interdependency and recognizing such relationships is valued at all levels in the organization.
- All team members are publically recognized for their achievements.
- Feedback is welcome and encouraged in all directions.
- All managers and leaders are visible and available.
- Resource utilization planning is ongoing and not just an annual talking point or task.
- Incorporating new or modifying existing processes happens constantly.
- A new or modified process has a goal that is tangible, practical, and achievable.
- Organizational potential is recognized and organizational performance is measured. The gap between is shrinking.
- When performance equals potential, new ways to increase potential are sought.
- Overall team performance is evaluated by team members. Non-performing members are coached or removed from the team.

- The concept that those team members doing the work are the ones that know how the work should be done.
- Managers are coaches and facilitators; they help to get tasks done but are not the reason for doing the tasks.
- Job satisfaction is high and moral is high.
- Team members desire to see that the organization's objectives are met and are committed to the group's success.

Cultivating Employee Commitment: Proactive and Innovative Team Members

Tony Blair, former British Prime Minister, stated, "...creativity and innovation are at the heart of a successful business."[3]

That statement can hardly be thought of as a new concept. Rather, successful businesses have always sought creativity and innovation in its employees. Think IBM, Motorola, Toshiba, and Panasonic; it was innovation and the creative genesis of their employees and engineers that allowed 100,000+ patents to be filed just by just these four companies. And this innovation was not just in new technologies. These companies were and still are leaders in systems processes and bringing products and services to the point of sale. This importance in innovation is even greater today for organizational success than it was two decades ago. Why is this?

WHY ARE PROACTIVITY AND INNOVATION IMPORTANT?

One reason is the decentralization that many organizations are now going to. More and more employees need to work without direct and close supervision. The better employees for these situations are those that are proactive and innovative. Another reason is that it is the employees that are closest to the

---

[3] "Blair Hails Millennium Products." BBC News. December 14, 1999. Accessed August 11, 2014.

customers that know the most about what is going on with the customers, customers' satisfaction, where problems in the systems are, and are the organizational face that the customer sees at the critical time in which the transaction happens. If organization is not listening to the current suggestions of their employees, then the organization is relying upon possibly outdated products and services and upon management's possibly dated, misconceived, and wrong perceptions. Third, proactivity and innovation promotes group success through their effects on employee results. Individual career success can translate into team performance and commitment. Employees that see their innovation rewarded are proactive toward more innovation. Finally, proactive and innovative employees are often more intrinsically motivated. Again, being allowed to be creative and being rewarded for that creativity leads to an inner enjoyment and more productive team member.

The problem is that most organizations are not very good at cultivating proactivity and innovations. According to a very recent study, "...companies focus too specifically on current goals and don't take the risks creativity requires"[4]

INCREASING PROACTIVITY AND INNOVATION WITHIN A TEAM

While most organizations are very good at evaluating the KSAs (knowledge, skills, and abilities) of their employees and candidates for employment, academic and practical research has shown that KSAs alone are not a solid indication of a person's proactivity and innovation. This research indicates that motivation and context (social, work, and organizational) are equally important in promoting innovation and proactivity within an individual.[5] These three different groups of

---

[4] "Rice U. Study: Creativity and Innovation Need to Talk More." *Rice University News*. April 8, 2014. Accessed August 11, 2014. http://news.rice.edu/2014/04/08/rice-u-study-creativity-and-innovation-need-to-talk-more/.
[5] Unsworth, Kerrie L. and Parker, Sharon (2003) Proactivity and Innovation: Promoting a New Workforce for the New Workplace. In: Holman, David and Wall, Toby D. and Clegg, Chris W. and Sparrow, Paul and Howard, Ann, (eds.) The New Workplace: A Guide to the Human Impact of Modern Working Practices. John Wiley & Sons,Chichester, pp. 175-196.

antecedents interact together to determine just how creative and inspired a team member is.

When speaking of KSAs, the greater understanding that an individual team member has of the process or system or task, the greater the likelihood that that team member will be proactive in making the process, system, or task work and work more efficiently. Organizational leaders and managers must be aware of the knowledge that their team members possess as well as making sure that the individual has the skill and ability to do the task. On a personal level, no one wishes to fail or to be seen in a negative light. Most of us will not place our self in a position in which, because of a limited knowledge or ability, possibly fail. The greater knowledge, the greater our confidence in what we are doing and willingness to do something we have not done before. Hence, a primary and continual task of organizational managers and leaders is the coaching, teaching, and facilitating of team members job knowledge, pertinent skills, and overall ability to perform within the organization.

Motivating team members is indispensable for any organization that desires to succeed. The difficulty facing managers and leaders that motivating a group of individuals is not a direct, easy-to-accomplish task. A group, of course, is a collection of diverse individuals with individual needs. To further complicate this mixture is that the individuals'' needs are in a constant flux of change. Organizations are also coming to realize that what might have once been a primary motivational factor (i.e. financial compensation) is no longer primary factor among more creative and proactive individuals. Recent studies have determined that organizational culture greatly influences individual team members' motivation.[6] Those organizations that emphasize more person-oriented in its corporative culture have more innovative employees than those organizations that are more task-oriented. (Person-oriented cultures emphasize developing individuals and individuals' works. Task-oriented cultures emphasize compensation promotion, status, and other traditional practices as motivating factors.)

---

[6] Helou, S., & Viitala, T. (2007). How Culture and Motivation Interacts.

Organizational Culture & Motivation

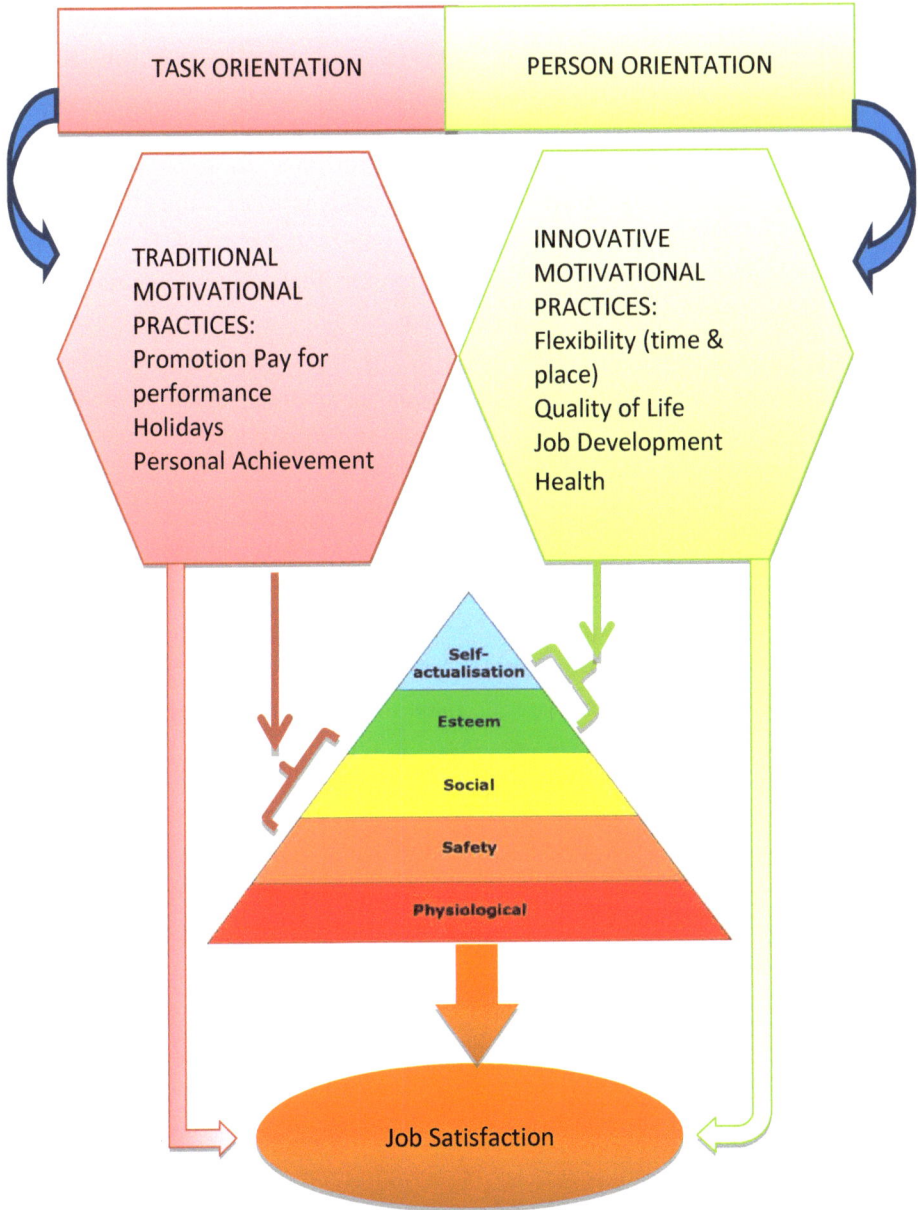

TASK ORIENTATION	PERSON ORIENTATION

TRADITIONAL MOTIVATIONAL PRACTICES:
Promotion Pay for performance
Holidays
Personal Achievement

INNOVATIVE MOTIVATIONAL PRACTICES:
Flexibility (time & place)
Quality of Life
Job Development
Health

Self-actualisation

Esteem

Social

Safety

Physiological

Job Satisfaction

While compensation and other traditional motivators may not be as strong in the younger generation of employees, these motivators remain connected to our individual need set. Thus, the most successful organizations may focus more on the proactive and innovative behaviors; however, they do not ignore or downplay the traditional motivators. The most successful organizations will cultivate a culture that combines task orientation and person orientation.

There are three sets of contextual factors that affect innovation and proactivity: task and work factors, social interaction characteristics, and the wider organizational context.[7] Probably the most important contextual factor is job autonomy and job complexity. The more autonomy that a team member has in completing a task, the more innovative that member is in finding a way to complete the task. None of us really enjoy having anyone standing over us while we are working. Autonomy contributes to a creative environment which increases innovation. Autonomy also increases a feeling of personal responsibility increasing both proactivity and innovation. Autonomy boosts self-efficiency, a sense of self-being, and a feeling of having control over one's task; all of which stimulate proactivity. Finally, autonomy adds to KSA acquisition which promotes the development of alternative processes and methods for task completion. One contextual factor that has proven to be very detrimental to innovation and proactivity is stress. In the context of job stressors, such as deadlines and excessive workloads, do not provide the team member with the opportunities to investigate alternatives or to increase KSAs.

Successful organizations deliberately include social interactions into their organizational culture schemes. Managers and leaders often expect and instruct team members to use their own initiative and judgement in doing their jobs. But when the team member behaves in an unexpected way, the manager or leader is shocked and expresses this shock to the team member. The team member will not only feel some resentment and confusion due to being considered as unproductive by the manager, but will also be much less likely to be innovative or proactive in the future. However, leaders and managers who inspire and enable

---

[7] Ibid. (Unsworth, Kerrie L. and Parker, Sharon)

creativity through words and actions and rewards increase the likelihood of innovative behaviors. The key is for leadership to avoid being too strong so as to suggest dominance or to behave contrary to verbal communication. Managers should be careful to resist change that innovation because innovation may involve changes to their roles and tasks.

Team members that feel safe in taking interpersonal risks, generally, will be more proactive and innovative. Employees do not wish to find themselves alienated from peers. Alienation causes distrust and lack of cohesiveness within a group. An employee's peers will often follow the projected attitude of managers and leaders toward coworker. The leadership of successful organizations is careful not to disengage team members even in instances of error or difficulties, personality conflicts. Leadership must maintain a personal ethos that does not communicate a disdain or problem with a particular employee. Additionally, organizations should be aware of the separations between work and job context and personal and home context. While no organization would want to be associated with criminal behavior of a team member, team members should not be made to feel that personality differences and personal preferences in private matters will cause them to be treated differently in the work place.

There is no doubt that some individuals that are more apt to be innovative and proactive due to their KSAs and personality. Obviously, organizations that desire an innovative workforce should make efforts to recruit such individuals into their teams. Amending or creating selection criteria that includes moving past technical skills to include assessing personal factors are paramount in recruiting self-starting innovators. However, this selection and recruiting is neither the sole nor even the best method to attain an innovative and proactive team. This error has proven to be very common in managers with the best intentions. Managers and leadership should focus on organizational strategies such as team and individual training and development. Innovation and proactivity both require superior levels of particular job and organizational knowledge and expertise. This knowledge and expertise is usually found within the current team membership. Second, it is not only possible, but it is easy to instill the more generic organizational ethos, skills, and motivation to active team members than the newly arrived. Third it is the active team members that already know the nuances of how the organization communicates, how it works, and its leadership functions.

Furthermore, there is very little reason for an organization to invest greatly into enlisting and/or developing innovative and proactive team members if the organizational culture does not permit proactive and innovative individuals if the environment does not allow, support, or promote innovation and proactive behavior. Organizations need to give attention to work context, organizational structure, and the organizations processes and methods for accomplishing tasks. Managers and leaders need to recognize that they do in fact influence the creativity and self-assurance of their employees.

Organizations need to design work and organizational structure that creates autonomous jobs that are challenging. Creating self-managing teams is an excellent strategy for coordinating groups whose members are interdependent upon each other. For individual tasks and jobs, permit the employees to self-manage as much as possible. Give the team member the power to make decisions that affect the outcome of their work. Managers should become facilitators rather than directors. But managers should also be careful that workloads and time expectations are realistic and do not create anxiety.

As organizations make these changes, it may become necessary for internal processes, work design, and organizational structure to be modified; such as changing the financial control systems so that the task-performing team members are not systematically blocked from making financial decisions regarding their tasks. Another example would simply allow team members a greater access to information so that they can work autonomously without continually going through management for needed the needed information.

Organizational design must support work context, task context and the recruiting, selection, and training of team members for innovation and proactivity to flourish. This design needs to facilitate team members' self-management and to employ cross-functional, interdepartmental, and inter-team cooperation. Job sharing, knowledge sharing, and even social events serve to better communication within teams and between teams and to allow individual team members to understand and to adopt the perspectives of others in the organization. However, organizational design is more than the existence formal systems, structures, and policies.   It is the informal characteristics of an organization that has proven to be more important in promoting innovation and proactivity than the formal policies and structures.

Developing an organization that truly promotes and supports innovative and proactive team members is not an easy accomplishment. That is why those companies that have achieved this feat have a competitive advantage.

Paying attention to, measuring, and controlling the important things

A very important method that managers and leaders use to communicate organizational ethics, principles, desires, and priorities are those things that these leaders pay attention to.[8] What a manager or leader emphasizes and measures over a longer period of time will have a profound influence on that organization's culture. This paying attention to certain things develops into a controlling method of communicating a message, particularly if the managers and leaders are thoroughly constant in their behavior. It is the uniformity that sends the message about the leaders' primacies, principles and beliefs. It is therefore the consistency that is most important and not the force of the action. Once team members place their attention on what their manager or leader is considering they begin to pay attention to that same thing. (All of us have a personal agenda, whether we admit it or not and our agendas can and will change. Sometimes our agendas are more or less selfish than at other times.) These agendas – these opinions, schemes, principles, concepts, and concerns – are items which leaders and managers wish to communicate.

The principles endorsed by a leader have weighty influence on the principles exhibited by the organization. Organizational managers and leaders play a key and very important part in establishing the ethos of their organization.   For

---

[8] Schein, E. M. (2004). *Organizational culture and leadership*. (3rd. ed.). Jossy-Bass.

16

example, a manager that pays great, perhaps too much, attention to document format creates the impression that the organization is more concerned with how something is presented than the substance or content of the communication.

Organizational managers and leaders utilize both positive and negative gestures as controls that draw the attention of team members to what is important to that manager or leader and that group or even the overall organization. Successful organizations develop within their cultural a reciprocal trust between the organization and its leaders and its team members. This trust is not only seen as morally and ethically correct, but it also promotes more open internal communications. Leader's that are always truthful consciously, and unconsciously through their behavior, tell their team members that honesty is valued within the organization. Likewise, leaders that display what their team member perceive as an ethical behavior can instill the idea that honesty is not really important to the organization. Having a stated business code of conduct is not enough; managers and leaders must present very strong gestures, paying attention in the direction of ethical behavior, and proactive in assuring organizational policies and procedures are adhered to all times. This paying of attention should include both the positive aspects of ethical behavior but also being consistent corrective and punitive measure should such be indicated. The behavior, the principles, the morals, and the attitude of the leaders are the most direct representation and reflection of an organization's culture. Paying attention to what the leader is paying attention to is the best indicator those leaders consider important.

Reacting to critical incidents and crises in the organization

Crises, due to their nature, attract the attention of all those nearby. Hence, those who are active in mitigating the crisis find themselves and their actions scrutinized by all observers. It is a leader's response and reaction during a crisis situation that is tale-telling about an organization's culture.

A crisis situation in an organization has a tendency to highlight organization's core values.

"...when an organization faces crises, the manner in which leaders and others deal with it creates new norms, values, and working procedures, and reveals important underlying assumptions."[9]

A crisis within an organization draws a large amount of attention from team members and external customers and often times emotional involvement from team members. This attention and emotional involvement is even greater if the existence of the organization is threatened. In a crisis, individual's and group deep-rooted values are open for observation and evaluation. Reactions are visible. It is during a crisis that any differences between the organization's espoused or stated values and the artifact values (the real, what-really-goes-on-here values) are exposed. Just as in our personal lives, it is a crisis that displays who and what an organization is all about. It is in the aftermath of an organizational crisis that leadership is uniquely set to either reinforce the existing organizational culture or to bring about changes within the culture. These survived organizational crises points can become a uniting event to improve the organization or they can be the harbingers of an organization's impending failure.

Allocating assets, rewards and status

The organizational budget is the primary tool for allocating the organization's resources. The manner in which leaders and managers allocate the available assets, through budgeting, provides a great insight into those leaders' and managers' expectations, convictions, and ideas. Academic business research has proven that it is the organization's leaders' beliefs about the importance or potential of a particular department, business unit, or aspect of an organization is the primary determining factor in budget line items.

However, this same research indicates that perceived inequities by team members when it comes to the budget can often will decrease overall organizational effectiveness.[10] It is with the equitable distribution of assets, the

---

[9] Ibid.

18

equal sharing of organizational rewards, and non-partisan granting of status that team members feel more part of the organization and more willing to invest themselves into the organization. Consequently, moral and ethical behavior increases.

It is also through performance appraisal that an organization can make a significant impact on its culture. Using the performance appraisal process to reward desired behaviors and also to punish undesired behaviors is common and acceptable. However, the organization needs to be sure that such rewarding or punishing is directly tied to behaviors and the results of those behaviors that are definitely within the scope of those members control. Organizations with more than one business unit may find that one units decrease in profitability is caused by the same factor that increases another units profitability. To punish that one will rewarding the other can seriously decrease team members' engagement. Performance appraisal should also be used to gauge the effectiveness of organizational change on a continual basis.

Organizations should develop a reward system when new knowledge or the more effective application of existing knowledge. Incentive pay and/or promotions are for such contributions are visible indications of a positive organizational culture. It is the linking of rewards to globally achievable goals that help to maximize team members' willingness to invest in their organization.

Being deliberate and thoughtful mentors, teachers, and coaches

Team members in an organization do not only listen to managers and teachers, they watch what that leader does. A leader sends very key and potent messages to team members through actions and behaviors, as we have already discussed. And as we know from personal experience, actions do speak louder than words.

---

[10] Thompson, A. A. , Strickland, A. J., Gamble, J. E. (2005). *Crafting and executing strategy: The quest for competitive advantage: Concepts and cases* (4thed.). McGraw-Hill, Irwin

Thus, leaders do a much greater job at teaching, coaching, and mentoring through their actions than through their verbal instruction.

In successful organizations, leaders and managers get out of their personal offices and cubicles and go to where the team members are working in order to mentor. And mentoring should be one of the primary tasks of a leader. Good leaders recognize that they are good, though they do not dwell in that knowledge. Dedicated and invested leaders want the organization to have other good leaders. So, who is best at developing good leaders? It is the present good and invested leaders who are best suited to grow and nurture good organizational leaders.

Organizational leaders should be not to simply reproduce themselves in their charges but to enable and encourage their charges to achieve greater success. Yes, that is a very hard thing to do, something that seems to go against the personal traits of successful persons. But we are talking organization. An invested and engaged leader wants what is best for the organization and not simply personal gain. The invested and engaged leader in a driven organization recognizes that what is good for the organization is good for the individual.

Additionally, leaders and managers are responsible for teaching team members what they need to know to do the job. We are not necessarily talking about the technical processes of completing a task; we are also talking about the organizational nuances. Managers and leaders may not be technically proficient over every concept and task of their team, but they should know who or where to find the technical expertise to teach a team member what is necessary to complete a task. These same managers and teachers should also know how to coordinate the all of the processes of their team to successfully complete the overall team objective. The engaged leaders will teach other team members what they know so that in order to increase overall team efficiency. This spreading and sharing of knowledge allows not only the leader opportunity to do more and to learn more but also empowers the team members with knowledge that they can build upon. Leaders and managers should be sure in letting team members know that just as team and individual assessment is an ongoing practice, so is learning and training and that perfection is not required while learning.

So how does an organizational culture encourage leadership to be more deliberate in coaching, teaching, and mentoring? Organizations should require that the leaders and managers get out of their offices and into the team's work areas.   Higher management can and should hold subordinate managers responsible for undue gaps in team knowledge. Providing adequate time in the leader's and manager schedule to teach and mentor is also essential. Organizations can also provide "train-the-trainer" type of training for managers and leaders. Policies and practices should promote verbal encouragement and hands-on teaching opportunities. Look for teaching moments and opportunities. Give the team members the opportunity to practice newly learned KSAs. And give team members the opportunity to achieve and to fail.   If someone feels that perfection is required at all times, then there will be great hesitance to do something new something that is yet unperfected. Rewarding the attempt to do something new, innovative, or proactive is just as important as rewarding success! Do not punish someone attempting something that is new for them even if after an unsuccessful attempt. Leaders and managers need to also control our natural inclination to have favorites. If not careful, leaders and managers may well find themselves spending a disproportionate of their time and efforts with a chosen favorite or two. Other team members cannot help but notice this behavior and so they will react, possibly in a negative manner, to what they perceive as an unjust favoritism. Yes, potential leaders and manages must be sought and recognized and these potential future leaders and managers will require additional mentoring over some other team members. However, care must be taken not to make other team members feel that their learning opportunities are being taken from them. Rather, engaged team members of the most successful organizations recognize individual talents and gifts in their coworkers and peers. They also understand that the success of those possibly more talented or differently talented individuals will have a very direct impact upon the organization's success and, in turn, their success.

A crucial issue is how learning is transferred to individuals within the organization. Formally communicating messages from leaders to team members is certainly a requirement within an organization.   However, informal communication, especially when teaching and mentoring, often times a more powerful tool. Informal communication lessens the chasm between leader and subordinate.

While the recognition between leader and subordinate is necessary at times, this chasm can also be hindrance to effective group task completion.

What about trust and communication?

> Communications can't make a person trust someone who is basically untrustworthy. But it can create a culture in which trust thrives.
> – Ivey Business Journal

Developing trust in an organization's leadership calls for an individual effort on the part of the leaders themselves. But it is a team effort also. The organizational function most likely to support the leaders' work and efforts to develop or maintain trust is communications.

Nearly all effective communication is a mixture of formal and informal communications methods.[11] Informal methods deliver more specific and more common instructions and direction in quickly addressing issues. Informal communication is usually more flexible. Lunch sessions and round-table discussions are much more valuable in getting a quick assessment or many workplace and group issues including trust and credibility. Open, informal communication has proven to be the best way of getting feedback from team members. Emails and telephone calls are excellent. But it is in a friendly, positive environment of face-to-face open communication that the most communicating usually takes place. While words say a lot, it is body language that indicates whether or not those words are believed or are credible.

Formal communication methods require more preparation and execution, but can be worth the effort. Focus groups and interviews with representative team members are excellent ways of obtaining feedback. When steered by an objective

---

[11] Beslin, Ralph, and Chitra Reddin. "How Leaders can communicate to Build Trust." *Ivey Business Journal*. November 1, 2004. Accessed August 13, 2014. http://iveybusinessjournal.com/topics/the-organization/how-leaders-can-communicate-to-build-trust.

facilitator or researcher, such sessions are able to include assessment exercises and sensitive, trust-related issues and topics.

Employee-driven/results oriented organizations

There is an old business maxim: *People don't leave companies, they leave bosses.* The foundation to this maxim is that if people are well managed, feel supported by leadership, and have challenging work assignments, obstacles can be overcome and great success can happen. It is the prospect of great success that draws the most talented and gifted people to an organization. And if the expected success is not delivered, these valuable people will not become engaged, invested, or stay with the organization. Managers and leaders at all organizational levels are responsible in delivering success and in engaging team members. These leaders must have support from an organizational culture that is performance-focused.

An organizational culture that cares and supports

Having an organizational competitive advantage rests more and more upon recruiting, choosing, engaging and retaining the best people – people who not only have the technical KSAs needed but also are very effective in leadership roles. But how do current leaders and managers make this happen in their organizations? Business academics now provide us with concepts and theories for in every area of business strategy; however, taking those theories and concepts and putting them to work has now become a major challenge in innovative organizational cultures. But the answer to this dilemma and challenge may well be simpler than we think. The most direct answer involves finding and developing supportive leaders.

The key global management trend is the concept that *Management will no longer be considered an art but will become a science.*[12] Science obliges fact-based

---

[12] McKinsey & Company, The McKinsey Quarterly, Member Edition, 5 January 2007

planning pointed at precise conclusions, pressed forward step-by-step with unhurried, careful testing. We have entered the time in which hiring, retaining, and promoting our team members is based upon what is proven and actually works time and again.

Every organization wants success. Success requires many things, and as mentioned above, talented, knowledgeable, and capable team members are primary to the success. Therefore, what is it that attracts, engages, and retains this kind of individuals that we want on our teams? What is it that defines and delineates a culture such individuals desire to be a part of? All individuals want the same things in the work place:

- to live their beliefs and accomplish their goals,
- to contribute in significant and innovative ways,
- to realize a rich connection between their personal contributions and the organization's vision,
- to be heard to and respected,
- to work for an organization recognized for outstanding customer care, and
- to have a life outside work.

So how does an organization help its people to achieve these things?

Research (science) in organizational effectiveness and business practice show us that an organizational culture which enables team members to achieve these goals must have leadership that is resilient, responsive, and emotionally competent. Emotional competence – being conscious of yourself and others, dealing with personal issues while also managing relationships with other – is one of today's primary leadership elements for business success.

Each day more and more business experts and academics cry for vendors to surrender control of their products and involve customers in dialogue. Company blogs, Facebook pages, and Tweets are happening with every increasing speed. But as these organizations boldly enter these new worlds, many if not most, still fail at adopting this practice of open dialogue in their internal communication processes with current and future employees. The outcome of this open-dialogue shortcoming the company's talking "at" team members rather than talking "with" its members. However, some organizations have learned that putting the employee first in the organization's culture allows, promotes, and creates unmatched customer service and in-turn, the success the organization hopes to achieve. These atypical companies have the philosophy that if given the freedom to create their own work environments, not only are the best team members recruited but they are retained. This exceptional team is a primary factor in exceptional success due to low staff turnover rates, innovative products and production processes, and happy team members that are motivated to provide the best customer service they can.

What creates an employee-driven organization? Having great perks and giving super gifts is not everything in a genuine employee-driven organization. Regrettably, countless organizations "gift" team members with a one-size-fits-all mentality without ever considering the individuality of its team members.

Employee-driven organizations are embedded in and stem from the organization's culture.   Countless organizations have a value statement that recites eloquently on paper, but does not work in practice.   A value statement may endorse the prominence of teamwork, but upon closer examination of the organization, we see that it is individuals rather than the team that receives the lion's share of the rewards. Questions to ask in determining if your organization is employee-driven:

- Do you track employee engagement, satisfaction and understanding and then act on the findings?
- How do you share your information and make decisions? Are your communications interactive or primarily top-down?
- Are your HR policies built on a philosophy of restricting, controlling and stopping behavior, or investing in ways to promote good behaviors that drive business objectives?
- Does your physical environment support positive employee interaction?[13]

---

[13] Barney, Christine. "Why Every Organization Should Embrace the Employee-Driven

There exist two organic barriers that inhibit the existence and creation of a genuine employee-driven organization. Organic because these barriers are rooted in personal traits that each person has to a degree and that each person must learn to overcome; these traits are natural to every individual and thus to every organization. Organizations, like the individual need to learn to bridle these two traits to a degree:

- **Lack of trust.** Respect and flexibility form the foundation of an employee-driven organization. If the leadership appears suspect of its team members then the work atmosphere will be one of distrust and fear. Employees do not want to be thought of as thieves, cheaters, or liars. Within reason and when possible, employees should be allowed to choose the location and hours of work and provide greater access to organizational resources. Now such arrangements do beg the question of how does management know if team members are actually working. The obvious answer to this question is twofold. First, each team within an organization needs to develop a method to track the time and productivity of each team member. The next higher management/leadership level, in turns, tracks the overall time and productivity of its subordinate team. Now, this is not adding to the leaders' workload as these functions should already be in place to monitor team effectiveness. Second, outcomes and results are the best indicators of proactivity. If the task is not being completed, or is being completed poorly, it will be found out quickly by the team members. In an employee-driven organization, slackers are usually first identified and addressed by other team members.
- **Desire for Control.** Team members are better able to contribute to the organization's success (read as profitability) when they not only understand what is going on around, beneath and above their work level, but also when they have some control over their work level. And being

---

Workplace" December 31, 2012. Accessed August 14, 2014.
http://www.rbbpr.com/news/76/Why-Every-Organization-Should-Embrace-the-Employee-Driven-Wo.aspx.

able to see and have some control where profits are invested, especially at their work level, is vital to team members' motivation. Many if not most workplace decisions are made backwards; that is financial consideration is given first priority rather than suitability or what is best for the task or process. No product is produced without customer or "user" input. Likewise, the team members that will be using the tool or process are the best suited to make many work place decisions. An employee-driven organization allows the team members to drive the decisions about processes, resources, and tools needed for the team's task completion. It is the scrutiny from daily using what is available that allows team members to know what will best serve them and what is the best investment of the organization's profits. The accounting and purchasing teams should support the teams' decision-making processes by opening the books to ensure the decisions do include monetary factors as well as task goals.

Developing, transitioning, or adopting an employee-driven/results oriented organizational culture is not easy nor is it initially inexpensive. Doing so requires patience, time, and money. However, the return on the investment of putting into place and maintaining practical, functional employee-driven/results oriented organization is can be enormous.

One example: Zappos

Zappos, the very successful online shoe and clothing company has a very unique organizational culture. One of the primary things that makes Zappos different is its ten core values and its recruiting, training, and retention processes that are aligned to these core values. Let's take a look at what Zappos appears to be doing correctly in its Human Resources department. But first the core values:

- "Deliver WOW Through Service
- "Embrace and Drive Change
- "Create Fun and A Little Weirdness
- "Be Adventurous, Creative, and Open-Minded

- "Pursue Growth and Learning
- "Build Open and Honest Relationships With Communication
- "Build a Positive Team and Family Spirit
- "Do More With Less
- "Be Passionate and Determine"
- "Be Humble"[14]

Zappos has a training team that focus in each core value. Each employee receives the same explanations of the values, and learns the behaviors that the employees are expected to live by each work day in the work place.

New hires at Zappos are courted rather than recruited. Many potential employees are identified then the members of the team that the potential employee would be working with meet the candidate at an informal gathering away from the workplace. After a period of time in which Zappos' employees have interacted in social settings is a decision to offer the potential employee a position with the company.

Though the courtship might not be as rigorous for every position, before any candidate is hired the candidate meets with several team members and will usually attend a department or company social event of some type. This social event attendance allows those team members who may be participating in the interview to meet the candidate informally.

Zappos takes organizational culture and employees that fit seriously. Several months may pass between the initial interview that focuses as much on cultural fit than anything else and a job offer. If a candidate does not pass the cultural fit initial interview, the candidate is not invited to meet another employee or the hiring manager. Zappos place more importance on cultural fit than any other recruiting factor.

---

[14] Heathfield, Susan. "Want to Know How Zappos Reinforces Its Company Culture?" January 1, 2014. Accessed August 13, 2014.

Interviewers have established five or six behavior based questions. These questions highlight a candidate's congruence with Zappos core values. This unique approach to interviewing permits interviewers to evaluate a candidate's likely or unlikely suitability within the culture and to display the essential skills.

Each interviewer provides particular feedback about candidates; some positions require a consensus from the interviewers while some are majority vote from interviewers. Interviewing team members' feedback consist of answering specific questions as well as open narratives of their opinions of the candidate's fit into Zappos' culture.

All new employees at Zappos spend their first three to four weeks working in the call center. The call center is the heart of the business and this is the heart of their customer service. All employees are expected to know how to give the best customer service. This approach also assures that there will be trained staff to maintain the call center even in the busiest times of the year. The company Zappos does not hire short-term employees for the busy seasons. All company employees are expected to work shifts in the call center during holidays and other busy times when extra help is needed. This initial training allows all team members to provide the desired customer service and technical expertise to keep the heart of the business functioning.

After completing their initial call center training time, the new employee is offered $3000 to resign from the company. Zappos feels that if you have not yet become a fit into the culture and adopted the company's goals, the company would prefer that you simply leave as employees that are not "sold out" to the company's core values will not be as productive as those who are.

Pay increases at Zappos are based upon learning new skills and developing additional abilities. Team members take and complete tests to receive raises. Raises and benefits are not dependent upon subjective reviews.

Every team manager is required to spend 10 to 20% of the department's time in time building exercises and activities. This large amount "social" time allows the team members to become more comfortable with the company's culture, with the other team members, and the company's core values. These activities are happen outside the workplace to further increase the core values validity.

Zappos managers do not do performance evaluations on team members. Rather managers conduct cultural assessments. These assessments provide feedback to the team member regarding their fit within the culture and how to improve.

Department managers are the ones that create career tracks within their respective departments, not senior management or Human Relations. There are two career paths in each department: a regular career path for most team contributors and a "super star" path for those members that excel. Living within the company's cultural norms is the key in career advancement and success

The call center team members do not work from scripts. They are expected to use their imagination in making customers happy. They are empowered to serve the customers and to give customers the "wow factor". And with more than 75% of total sales coming from repeat customers, they are obviously succeeding.

It appears that not only has Zappos discovered that team members' fitting into an organization's culture is a primary factor for organizational success, but they have also found some unique ways of finding those individuals they feel are of the right mix. Assuring that there is a continual meshing of individual's values into the company's values also appears to be something that many organizations should do more of.

Another example with a different approach: Google

Google, the number three most valuable company in the world as of 2013, is a people-driven/results oriented company.[15] Google and its advocates acknowledge profess a new path has become evident to corporate success and greatness. Organizations and companies that are following this "new path" are dominating their competition through continuous innovation and great leaps in

---

[15] Sullivan, John. "How Google Became the #3 Most Valuable Firm by Using People Analytics to Reinvent HR". EREnet. February 25, 2013. Accessed August 14, 2014.

innovation. Organizational leaders are learning that this innovation cannot happen until an organization deliberately focuses toward its people and team members.

Focusing strategically on people and managing people, as we have already discussed, is necessity for innovation simply because innovation comes from people. Recruiting and retaining innovators is a prerequisite for innovation. Further, great innovators need to have great leaders and managers as well as a workplace environment that is conducive to innovation. Regrettably, making the shift to an innovative organization is challenging because nearly every present HR task functions under the 20th century ideologies of historical practices and measures of efficiency, risk evasion, legal compliance, and people management decisions that are based upon hunches and guesses. Google's stance is that if you desire extreme innovation, you will need to reinvent HR from the traditional processes that dominate most HR departments into a department that is also driven by innovation.

Google uses what it calls a "people analytics" approach to its people management. The basic idea of this approach and tactic is that precise people management judgments are the most vital decisions that an organization can make. It is impossible to create or have superior business success unless your leaders and managers are making correct people management decisions. Many detractors of Google and the people-oriented organizational culture argue that it is research and development, resource allocation or marketing are more important and influential in business decisions. However, the fact is that every business decision is made by team member that is breathing, thinking, feeling; that is a person. By hiring and retaining mediocre people and provide little data, you must assume that these people will only make mediocre decision in these business situations as well as in people management. Googles' take is that no organization would allow its finance, or purchasing, or marketing or other business unit to offer a solution to a problem or task without as much varied and pertinent data being collected and analyzed as possible. However, HR, in most organizations is relies more often than not on trust and relationships. Google has said that this difference in decision-making tools between HR and the other business units needs to be reduced. Moreover, people costs (compensation, benefits, recruiting, training, etc.) often reaches 60% of an organization's variable costs. It simply makes sense to Google to manage this major cost item analytically.

Human Resources in the Google organization is radically different all other HR functions. To begin with, it is not referred to as human resources; rather it is called "People Operations". The business unit itself has been elevated to a level in which an organizational vice-president heads the unit rather than a lower or mid-level manager. The unit's working paradigm is to mandate data-based decisions to all of the organizational units that it supports. People management decisions within Google are steered by the influential "people analytics team." Two quotes from this team speak to the team's goals and task:

- "All people decisions at Google are based on data and analytics"
- The goal is to ... "bring the same level of rigor to people-decisions that we do to engineering decisions"[16]

Google is replacing as much of the traditional subjective decision-making style in HR. This new approach style maybe called "people analytics" it is referred to and described by its academic proponents as 'data-based decision-making, "fact or evidence-based decision-making, and "algorithm based decision-making.

The people analytics team reports directly to the VP and it has a representative in each major HR function. It produces many products, including employee surveys that are not anonymous, and dashboards. It also attempts to identify insightful correlations and to provide recommended actions. The goal is to substitute data and metrics for the use of opinions.

The special perks and social, fun activities (i.e. free food, 20% time, and subsidized massage therapy) are well known. But most people do not realize that each of these perks have been put in and kept in place due to data. Google has determined that these perks contribute to the overall success of the company and

---

[16] Ibid.

contribute to the bottom line profits. Unique approaches to Google's people analytics include:

- Leadership traits and managerial roles. While it has always been held that superior managers will usually produce better production, Google's "Project oxygen" analyzed vast amounts of internal data. There now proven results proved that the better the manager, the better performance of the team and the greater retention of innovative team members. The research project also pin-pointed eight traits of superior leaders. In order of importance, those traits are:
    1. Be a good coach.
    2. Empower; don't micromanage.
    3. Be interested in direct reports, success and well-being.
    4. Don't be a sissy: Be productive and results-oriented.
    5. Be a good communicator and listen to your team.
    6. Help your employees with career development.
    7. Have a clear vision and strategy for the team.
    8. Have key technical skills so you can advise the team.[17]

It should be noted that the most important traits are social people traits. The least import trait is technical traits. Google's VP for People Operations said when asked about technical skills in a high-tech company, "It turns out that that's absolutely the least important thing. Much more important is just making that connection and being accessible."[18] Google's managers are assessed twice a year on these eight characteristics.

This same research identified three major and common managerial snares:

1. Trouble making a transition to the team.
2. Lack of a consistent approach to performance management.

---

[17] Hall, Brad. "Google's Project Oxygen Pumps Fresh Air Into Management." The Street. February 11, 2014. Accessed August 14, 2014.
[18] Ibid.

3. Spending too little time managing and communicating.

These pitfalls are common in those managers who continue to act as technical experts rather than team leaders. The representative behavior of these "too busy to manage" managers was, "This person is 'not proactive; waits for the employee to come to them.'"

- The PiLab. The PiLab is very unique to Google. This group conducts practical experiments within Google's teams to determine the most effective methods for managing people and continuing a productive environment. These experiments include discovering what type of reward makes the employees the happiest. The PiLab was able to contribute to better employee health, thus reducing sick time, by instructing the company's eating facilities to serve lower calorie meals. The Google gathered data and experiments showed that by simply reducing the size of the servings that caloric intake was reduced but that the individual was still content as the choices remained as before.

- A retention algorithm. Google developed a mathematical algorithm to proactively foresee and which team members are more likely to leave the organization. Using this approach, management is able to better engage the individual employees and to do so sooner, thus, heading off many retention problems.

- Predictive modeling. Members of the People Operations unit at Google are continually asking the question "what if". This proactive, forward looking approach, predictive models are developed which allows for better forecasting of and resolving people management problems.

- Improving diversity. Google uses analytics to resolve diversity problems in its team makeup. The people analytics team analyzed data to identify the underlying causes of ineffective recruiting, the retention of, and the promoting of certain social groups; women engineers were one of these groups.

- An effective hiring algorithm. Google developed an algorithm, based upon research, which allowed for the predicting of candidates that had the higher probability of success if hired. This research also indicated that there was very little to no value going beyond four candidate interviews. This knowledge significantly shortened the hiring time for many positions. Google also uses groups to make hiring decisions as this prevents managers from hiring based upon their own short-term goals.

- Calculating the value of top performers. The people operations professionals at Google calculate the differential in performance between average technologists and exceptional technologists. Sometimes this difference is 300 times higher. Being able to show the value of top talent persuades managers and executives the wisdom in providing resources needed to recruit, develop, and retain the most talented team members.

- Workplace design drives collaboration. Being deliberately fun and managing "fun" may seem superfluous to many organizational managers, but not at Google. Data indicates that having fun is a major issue in recruiting, retention, and in group cooperation. Data also shows that innovation is increased with discovery and learning, with group cooperation, and with fun. Google designs its workplace environments to maximize innovative thinking.

- Increasing discovery and learning. Google emphasizes hands-on learning rather than classroom learning. Once again, this is due to data. The huge majority of all people learn quicker and better through on the job/hands-on learning. Google rotates team members through different projects, and not punishing earnest, but unsuccessful new ventures as methods to increase discovery and learning. Bringing in outside speakers such as Al Gore and Lady Gaga, while perhaps not technical masters, do provide opportunities for entertainment, getting away from a desk, and for learning something from a different professional discipline.

- Google does not dictate; Google convinces with data. The final key factor to Google's people analytics success happens when the team makes it presentations and proposals to the managers, leaders, and executives. The team assumes the role of consultants to advice rather than to demand or force. The team answers questions, gives recommendations and presents the data to support those answers and recommendations. As the team's audiences are very analytical, (and most organizational executives are analytical), this presented data

35

changes pre-established opinions and influences decisions to be more objective.

Google has also taken an innovative approach to innovation. While recognizing that establishing goals is critical to the any organization's success, Google does not necessarily seek continual improvement. Again, using data, Google has found that 6 Sigma and other well-intentioned continuous improvement goals may actually reduce innovation within companies, teams, and individual. Rather than seeking small incremental increases in innovation and improvement, pursue large advances that completely reestablish product and service boundaries and standards. Larry Page, Google's CEO, set an extraordinary goal for his team members to create "products and services that are 10 times better than the competition." He explains that a "...1,000% improvement requires rethinking problems entirely, exploring the edges of what's technically possible, and having a lot more fun in the process."[19]

Google has determined that organization's often set goals that that are too low and that things are made worse by actually achieving those lowly goals.

Changing HR

Existing companies that are not growing should consider that your company's current HR practices, policies, and operations are actually restricting your firm's growth. Chances are that your company has not yet made the shift from the traditional subjective hiring and promoting exercise to more objective approaches that have proven to produce higher results and returns on personnel investments.

Regrettably, most senior managers, leaders, and executives, including HR leaders, are unaware of the analytical approach to people management that is becoming more and more available each day. (Without attempting to sound too tongue-in-cheek google "people analytics software" to see what is happening in this quickly growing arena.) However, once executives comprehend this analytic approach to

---

[19] Ibid. Sullivan.

36

HR they see that it coincides with the way decisions are made in all other major business functions. But again, like in all human endeavors, there are some obstacles. Many HR professionals are lacking in the technical areas of analytics, statistics, and mathematics. And there are many, many HR traditionalists that simply resist these changes because they are uncomfortable with learning and with innovation and just do not want to reinvent what they already do. But are they doing what they do in the best that it can be done?

Talent Magnets

Zappos, Google, Apple, Eastman Chemical, Nestle-Purina, Orbitz are talent magnets. And this attraction is not only in the job classifications that these companies are known for. Less than 40% of Google's employees are software engineers. These companies are hiring the best talent, the most innovative talent in a wide range of business job categories.

These companies are successful because they attract and retain excellent talent. They are able to expand as they do because they can attract excellent talent in any and all job families. They are known for treating their employees well.

Even more interesting is that if when we look at Google and Apple and others, we see that their success was not immediate. It happened after they made the conscious shift to become innovative companies and to become talent magnets. These companies, Google and Apple in particular, rose from the bottom of their competitive landscapes to having product and service dominance over their competition within a decade. Assuming that this success is due to their infrastructure of buildings and equipment and attempting to replicate that infrastructure may help some, but it will not get you very far. It requires the right people in those buildings and using that equipment in innovative ways to be successful.

The game has changed, and it is no longer the largest or oldest firms that win. Instead, it is the firms with the most innovators that win. And in the future, that need for innovators will only increase.

The Most Important Secret to a Successful Organizational Culture

Trust.

That's it. Nothing fancy. Nothing complicated. Very basic. Very fundamental.

Trust is the primary, basic, first quality/trait/characteristic/principle/concept that puts Google, Zappos, Southwest Airlines, Facebook, Orbitz, and the other corporate list leaders on those lists.

Organizations that trust their team members to work as expected, not to take advantage or cheat the company, not to undermine their peers, not to booby-trap their managers, and that such behavior is not only ultimately detrimental to their own success as well as the corporate success, are going to attract individuals that live this life ethos. And what individuals are most content, most happy, and, hence, more innovative and procreative?? The very clear answer is those of us that show and display trust in those around us. Those of us who practice the principle all are innocent until proven guilty have much less to worry about and to inhibit our thinking and to occupy our thinking time than those who feel they have to defend everything they have against every person in the room with them.

One can find countless and varied definitions of trust the academia of organizational culture. But all of these different definitions discuss similar, intangible characteristics of human behaviors.

Trust is commonly described as:

- "The belief in the integrity, character, and ability of a leader."[20]

---

[20] S.P. Robbins and M. Coulter, *Management* (6th ed.), Prentice Hall, 1999

- "Reciprocal faith in one's intentions and behaviors."[21]
- "A confidant reliance on the integrity, honesty, or justice of another."[22]

Justice, honesty, reliability, faith, ability, character, and integrity are words that sometimes prove to be difficult to live up to in the modern workplace. However, it is these high moral and ethical standards that create an organizational culture of trust.

> "Trust men and they will be true to you; treat them greatly, and they will show themselves great."
>
> --Ralph Waldo Emerson

The concept of organizational trust can be used in various ways in today organizational landscapes. There is the trust that one organization has in another organization; perhaps we can refer to this as interorganizational trust. An example of this is an organization's trust in FedEx to delivery necessary documents timely and securely. There is also intraorganizational trust; a trust that focuses upon the relationships between teams, other teams, those teams' immediate and senior managers and leaders. Then we have interpersonal trust; the trust found within groups and between individual members of teams and their immediate peers.[23]

The Types of Trust

Just as not every type of trust is beneficial in a personal relationship, the same is true for workplace relationships. Four types of trust have been identified and described:

---

[21] R. Kreitner and A. Kinicki, *Organizational Behavior* (4th ed.), Irwin McGraw-Hill, 1998

[22] Funk and Wagnalls, *Standard Desk Dictionary*, Harper & Row, 1985.

[23] K.T. Dirks, "The Effects of Interpersonal Trust on Work Group Performance," *Journal of Applied Psychology*, Vol. 84, 1999, pp. 445-455

- Basic trust is the capability and inclination to meet people without unwarranted suspicion, the ability to chat comfortably to and interact with strangers, and the readiness to enter into close relationships. Basic trust offers the base for one's whole personality and character toward the world.
- Simple trust is the total absence of suspicion: it seeks no thinking, no conscious choice, no analysis, and no reasoning. It may be present because the trusting person has no reason to doubt the other's trustworthiness, but it may be present because the trusting person is simply naïve.
- Blind trust occurs when one has experienced a violation or betrayal at the hands of another, but refuses to believe or accept that the violation or betrayal has occurred. One who has blind trust denies that the trusted party would ever do anything that would even do something to untrustworthy.
- Authentic trust is conscious, sensible, and fully self-aware of its own surroundings and boundaries, and is open to growth. Authentic trust is grounded on choice and accountability rather than the perfunctory operations of following rules, reliability, and predictability. Authentic trust is very cognizant of the perils and is willing to confront wariness and overcome it.

Authentic trust stimulates productive and dynamic organizational relationships. An authentic trusting relationship does not happen by chance, nor can it be delegated, forced, or mandated. Authentic relationships develop over time, beginning with small events and continuing to full strength grounded on the total of individual's experiences. Building such an affiliation in the workplace is a shared process where both the team member and the manager/leader willingly assumes the responsibility for creating, building, and maintaining trust through high levels of regard, respect, and esteem.

Benefits of Trust

It has been shown through numerous studies that organizations with high levels of cultural trust are able to recruit, develop, and retain team members that are innovative and proactive.[24] These team members are more apt to enjoy their work, to do their jobs more correctly and efficiently, be willing to take risks, to embrace the organization's values and goals, and to exhibit overall behavior that is congenial, helpful, and fruitful to peers and to the team. This positive inclination allows managers and leaders more time and freedom to coach, teach, and mentor.

Organizational trust also provides the benefit of perceived justice within the organization. When team members have a trust in and within the organization the team members perceive fairness exists also. Team members perceive that they are and will be treated fairly and justly within the organization. They also perceive that they are and will be compensated fairly for their efforts. And they perceive that the success of the organization will be distributed fairly and justly throughout the organization. Again, this perceived justice promotes innovative and proactive behavior in team members.

Barriers to Developing an Organizational Culture of Trust

Team members, policies, and practices often act as barriers to developing trust as well as creating breaches of trust. A few situations that organizational leaders should be aware of and to proactively avoid when attempting to establish organizational trust are:[25]

---

[24] R. B. Shaw, *Trust in the Balance: Building Successful Organizations on Results, Integrity, and Concern*, Jossey Bass, 1997.
[25] R. Galford and A. Seibold Drapeau, *The Trusted Leader: Bringing Out the Best in Your People and Your Company*, The Free Press, 2002.

- Team members that have personal agendas and desires for elevation, control, and acknowledgement that do not align with the organization's values and strategies.
- Team members with unstable personalities that reveal a want for vengeance.
- Team members that intentionally muddle and confuse communication channels.
- Team members that are incompetent or perceive their peers, leaders or managers to be incompetent.
- An organizational history of underperformance, multifarious situations, numerous reorganizations, countless management changes.
- Organizations with inflexible, erratic, unreliable, unpredictable organizational practices, policies and standards.

In order to overcome these barriers, the organization must use strong, convincing leadership prove that that these barriers are being dealt with.

How to Develop an Organizational Culture of Trust

Continuous change and improvement occurs in an organization with a high degree of trust. Organizations that cultivate the needed high level of trust for the needed change, innovative and proactive team members, and organizational improvement include the following practices in their organizational cultures:[26]

- Having humane leadership. Confirm to employees know you are mindful of, sensitive to, and sympathetic of their distinct feelings, thoughts, and experiences. Reassure them that promises will be kept, confidences kept, and sensitive information handled carefully.
- Being a model of trustworthiness. Be honest by not only saying what will be done but having the integrity to do what was said would be

---

[26] S. Sendjaya and J. Sarros, *Servant Leadership: Its Origin, Development, and Application in Organizations*. Journal of Leadership and Organizational Studies, Vol. 9, 2002, pp. 57-64.

done. Show credibility by following through with commitments and verifying that commitments were completed by all involved.

- Having the willingness to recognize, to accept responsibility for, and to restore perceived breaches or betrayals of trust with team members.
- Developing, communicating, and applying organizational values and goals to confirm likeminded beliefs and a common focus on the tasks at hand. Integrate trust objectives into the organizational values and strategic plans.
- Determining if organizational procedures, policies, and rules are consistently applied justly, fairly and equally.
- Opening organizational communication networks by employing open-door and open-book policies and creating user-friendly networks. Share the findings of organizational assessments of task or process effectiveness with employees to show a culture of openness.
- Demonstrating faith in team members by reducing supervision. Allow team members to delegate team authority, responsibility and the workload within their teams.
- Providing work area environments that encourage collaboration but yet provide for personal identities.
- Investigating why problems and failure occurred rather than who is responsible.

Trust forms the groundwork for real communication, team member retention, motivation and input of discretionary energy – call it the extra effort – which team members voluntarily invest into their work. When trust subsists in an organization or in a relationship, almost everything else is easier to accomplish and more comfortable in achieving.

The Decision-Driven Organization

Why is it that almost half of all new CEOs launch company reorganizations within the first couple of years of their taking over the company? The answer is pretty simple; they would like to see better performance. But the problem is that less than one-third of all reorganizations actually create better performance.

Often times CEOs assume that the boxes and lines on the company's organizational chart as the primary determining factor of the company's financial performance. Like the general of an army, the CEOs views their task as placing the best collection of colonels, majors, and captains in the right places on the chart. For example, if the job facing the organization is to have greater innovation, than the CEO's task is to create the best organizational structure in order to best channel organizational resources in the direction of innovation.

But if we look at the field general's organization and the origination's operations, we find that even with the best strategic resource system, the battle will be lost if good tactical decisions are not made by the officers and soldiers that are not only part of the resource system but, more importantly, upon those that are closer to the fighting. Despite common belief, the performance of an organization is not based solely upon the organization's physical resources. An organization's structure will only support increased performance if the organization's capability to make decisions and then to execute those decisions more quickly and with better effectiveness than its competitors.

For many, if not most organizations, this moving from a resource centric or task centric structure to a decision-making structure and culture requires a fundamental shift in thinking. While a strength, weakness, opportunity, and threat analysis (SWOT) is the usual first step in creating an organizational structure, decision-driven organizations begin with a decision audit. The objectives of the decision audit are for the leaders to grasp and comprehend the set of decisions that are vital to the success of the organization's strategic success. The audit also determines at what organizational level these decisions are best to be made and executed so the maximum value and effectiveness can be achieved.

The organization that can best align its structure with its decisions will have a great advantage over an organization that relies only upon its resources.

But as we look at organizational structure, we need to be aware that organizational structure is not the only element that determines performance. Many times it is not even the most important; but it is always a factor that should be considered when assessing strategic goals.

A Reality Check: Who's Making the Decisions and Why?

When an organization struggles, the guilt is often placed on something or someone outside of the organization. These faults and given reasons that are often cited are economic downturn, government regulations, or competition that has a greater geopolitical advantage, all factors that are beyond the organization's control. This is the conventional wisdom. However, reality and historical analysis of organizational failures in almost every instance had little to do with external market forces. Rather the culprit was almost always poor decision making regarding factors and elements within the control of the organization itself.

This fact is and of itself a startling realization that many organizational leaders may attempt to deny. This is not good! This fact underlines the vital importance of making good decisions in a timely manner. For any company to outdo its competition and to gain and maintain market leadership, the company must have a decision-making process that not only is fact-based but also flexible enough to allow decisions to be made quickly.

As we discussed in the previous sections of this book, driven organizations that are successful will have talented teams. These talented team members will be innovative and proactive. The organization will be able to and should have trust in these team members. So why should an organization not allow these team members to have input into decision making and even to allow them decision-making authority? Why should organizational senior leaders be using this pool of talented, motivated, and engaged team members in helping them, the senior leadership, to make better decisions?

A study by one of the world's largest and most successful business systems, management, and technology companies found two distinguishing behaviors in businesses that should be growing but were not.[27] The first damaging behavior is leadership's focusing and amplifying the positive while downplaying and discounting the negative. The research discovered manifold instances of senior leadership that gave very high marks to the decision making and their job performance; however, when subordinate managers and leaders and third-party contributors who actually executed those same rated decisions, there was a large gap in the performance ratings. The subordinates rated the senior decision-makers performance much lower because they saw the positive and the negative in what actually happened when the decisions were put into motion

The second behavior was the setting of bold goals and relying on unprecedented resource allowance to accomplish those goals without having sufficient empirical data and information to justify the goals or the risk. Basically, senior management often allows gut instinct to trump sound judgement and evidence. The study showed that decision-makers do not use the data in hand in an optimal fashion, they do not collaborate with the experts within their organizations as they should, and they do not use their existing analytical tools to make fact-based decisions. Yet, many of these senior leaders feel that they are making decision based upon full knowledge and understanding of all the relevant information.

It appears as if there is a major shortfall of collaboration within organizations.

Collaboration in a Decision-Driven Organization

Savvy organizations will make a fundamental shift, a shift that will be another competitive advantage, in the way its leaders perceive, use, and manage collaboration within their teams. In this organizational structure, team members are not just connected but they will be empowered and encouraged to make and

---

[27] Bradley, Joseph, Jeff Louks, James Macaulay, and Andy Noronha. Decision-Driven Collaboration. San Jose, California: Cisco Business Solutions, 2012.

to execute better decisions. This structure manages team member connections, it encourages collaboration between teams in all directions, it requires leaders to listen to their subordinates and to act upon what those subordinates have to say, it makes strategic use of human and information assets. However, this structure does not promote "committee decision-making". Decisions are still made by qualified individuals, but these individuals have increased intelligence in order to make the necessary decisions.

There are three central elements to structuring an organization for decision-driven collaboration:

- Engagement: Identify key team members and other experts, solicit their input, and share their ideas. Identify the team members who will be charged with evaluating all the information and making the final decision. Ideally this will be same person. It should be noted that this step is one that is common in organizational structures. The problem is that sharing ideas is only the first step in collaboration.
- Evaluation: Determine the question that needs to be answered and consider feasible alternatives. Once objectives of the decision have been established and the right team members and experts have been identified, then collaboration on the decision begins. Asking for alternatives from those team members and experts is crucial. Leadership should be geared to providing the experts with data access and resources needed to prove well-researched, viable options. Once those options have been presented and analyzed, then the decision-makers can select the best option.
- Execution: Make a defined decision, engage the relevant team members needed to execute the decision, and then put the decision into practice. Executing a decision requires the most collaboration. Once the alternatives have been studied the decision is made. The decision should be clear to all who have collaborated thus far. In many situations, executing the decision may include brining in new team members. These new team members must be engaged. As they may have ideas on how to execute their assigned tasks, collaboration must happen with them, also. And as nearly every original plan and decision will change after its

first trial, new learning and revision occurs.   The goal of productive execution is a continual circle of execution, learning, and revision.

We, once again, should note that Decision-driven collaboration does not require changes to the actual structures of an organization.   It does not mean that authority is shifted or diffused.   Actually, clear, distinct authority hierarchies remain vital to strong execution of decisions.

Organizational leaders   need to recognize that each team member is a decision maker. No, not all decisions are created equal. Some decisions have potential to fundamentally alter the direction of the organization, for good or for bad; whereas others do not.   But it is not only the big decisions that matter.   All decisions made by all team members, in total, have enormous weight in the success or failure of the organization.   Even the "smaller" decisions impact the operations and efficiency of the organization and the organization's ability to recognize a change in the market.

Collaboration allows the organization to focus in increasing the quality of each decision taken. This is done by creating a structural model that provides the team members with the needed tools, the data, the processes, and the interactions needed to engage, evaluate, and execute in every facet of their task completion. For the organization, collaboration in making decisions, large and small, allows for fact-based, informed, and more effective decisions.

Characteristics of a decision-driven organization

The significant characteristic of high-performing, decision-driven organization is its capability to make good decisions quickly and to make those decisions **happen** quickly. Organizations that consistently display high-performance nearly always follow a set of defined doctrines.

- **Some decisions are more important than others.** The decisions that matter most are those that are vital to building value in the organization. Some of these decisions are the big strategic ones. However, the less dramatic operating decisions that keep the organization running each day are just as important. These are the decisions that allow for effective execution of the strategic decisions.
- **The goal of all decisions is action.** Making a decision is not the end; rather implementing the decision is the goal. But even that is not the final goal. With each implementation, opportunities to make better decisions should present themselves. And consensus should not be a requisite for making a decision as this could become an obstacle.
- **Ambiguity should be avoided.** Accountability is vital. Determining who contributes information and expertise, who the decision-maker is, and who will be executing the decision should never be in doubt. These roles must be defined and communicated throughout the parties involved. Without this clear defining of roles, delay and gridlock will probably occur. But this clarity does not require concentrating authority in only a few people. It means that all involved knows who has the responsibility to make the decision, who will be having input, and who will be carrying out the decision.
- **Swiftness and flexibility are crucial.** The ability to make good decisions quickly allows an organization to capitalize on more opportunities and to overcome obstacles with greater ease. The best decision makers promote an environment in which team members come together rapidly and efficiently. They are practiced in making decisions and doing those decisions.
- **Decision-making roles overrule the organizational chart.** No organizational structure will be perfectly arranged for every decision.

49

The key is make sure that the right people are involved in the right level of the decision =making process at the right time.

- **The organizational structure reinforces roles.** Defined roles in the decision-making process are crucial, that is not enough. The organization must reinforce correct decision making through the flow of information, providing incentives, and through measurement of decision effectiveness. With this reinforcement, the desired behavior will become routine.

- **Doing beats talking.** Engage team members who will be working within the decision roles by having them to participate in designing the roles. When the team member is thinking about the new behaviors required to make and to execute the decisions, they are already beginning to adopt those new roles for themselves.

The Strategy-Focused Organization

An academic study of 275 expert portfolio executives reported that the capacity to implement strategy was more essential than the quality of the strategy itself.[28] Strategy execution was the most significant aspect shaping these portfolio executives' assessment of organization and corporate evaluations. This judgment seems astounding as for many years conventional wisdom, organization theorists, business advisors and the business media have fixated on how to develop strategies to produce greater performance. Seemingly, strategy making has never been more imperative.

Nevertheless, other observers concur with the portfolio executives' view that the capability to implement strategy can be more imperative than the strategy itself. One review of organizational business consultants reported that less than 10 percent of efficiently framed strategies were implemented effectively.[29] A Fortune magazine piece, a cover story of prominent CEO disappointments, determined that the weight placed on strategy and vision formed an erroneous belief that the correct strategy was all that was required to flourish. The authors concluded that "...in the majority of cases—we estimate 70 percent—the real problem isn't [bad strategy]...it's bad execution."[30] Therefore, with indicated failure rates in the 70 – 90% range, one can appreciate why shrewd investors have decided that strategy implementation is more vital than good vision.

Implementing Strategy: Why so difficult?

Strategy expert Michael Porter labels the foundation of strategy as the "activities" in which an organization selects to shine. If the base of strategy is, as Porter continues, the "selection and execution of hundreds of activities," then strategy

---

[28] "Measures That Matter," Ernst & Young, Boston, 1998
[29] Walter Kiechel, "Corporate Strategists Under Fire," Fortune, Dec. 27, 1982
[30] R. Charan and G. Colvin, "Why CEOs Fail," Fortune, June 21, 1999

cannot be restricted to a limited number of individuals at the upper echelons of an organization[31].

Strategy needs be comprehended and executed by every team member. The entire organization must be aligned around the organization's strategy, and performance management and measuring systems help produce that alignment. Here lies one of the chief causes of poor strategic managing. Most performance management and measuring systems are designed and around budgets and operating plans. They encourage short-term, incremental, tactical actions. Although this is an indispensable part of management, it is not sufficient. You cannot achieve strategy with a system planned for tactics. It is this requirement—the requirement for strategic organizational management—that has been motivating the pervasive acceptance of the Balanced Scorecard.

A Different Approach to Implementing Strategy: The Balanced Scorecard

The simple notion behind the Balanced Scorecard Concept (BSC), first introduced in a 1992 Harvard Business Review article, is that an organization's strategy needs to be converted into terms that can be comprehended and acted upon.[32] A BSC utilizes the language of quantity to more clearly define the meaning of strategic conceptions like quality, customer satisfaction and growth. A scorecard that precisely defines the strategy can assist in establishing framework for the organizational structure.

Organizations that adopted the Balanced Scorecard have shown impressive results to date. Consider the following case studies and the wide range of products and services they provide indicating that the BSC and strategy focused

---

[31] Michael Porter, "What Is Strategy," Harvard Business Review, November/December 1996
[32] R. Kaplan and D. Norton, "The Balanced Scorecard: Measures That Drive Performance," Harvard Business Review, January/February 1992.

organizational structure can work across many industries and types of organizations[33]:

Mobil Oil. The company began using the BSC in 1993 to help accomplish Mobil's conversion from a production-driven, highly-centralized, petroleum company to a customer-driven, decentralized, retail organization. The effects were quick and profound. By 1995, Mobil had progressed from last place to first place for profitability in the petroleum industry. It preserved this No. 1 place for five consecutive years, until its merger with Exxon in October 1999.

Cigna Insurance. Cigna also began using the BSC system in 1993. In 1992 Cigna P&C was the least profitable company in its insurance industry sector. A new CEO introduced the BSC to aid in managing Cigna's renovation from a money-losing general insurance company to an extremely profitable insurance sector specialist. The BSC allowed Cigna to focus on those niches where Cigna had a qualified competitive advantage. Again, the results were quick and impressive. Within two years, Cigna had reverted to profitability. This performance continued for four consecutive years. In 1998, Cigna P&C's profitability was in the top 25% of the entire insurance industry. The company, on the verge of bankruptcy five years before was sold for more than $3 billion in 1998.

Rockwater Energy Solutions. The company president introduced the Balanced Scorecard to the managing team in 1993 to help explain a recent merger of two acquired engineering corporations and increase consensus on the strategy for now organizations. The new strategy transformed the company from one contending solely on price and the marketing of engineering hours on construction projects into a corporation that could convey price centered on the value it added to its targeted clients. The scorecard-design method led to staffing a new management team, identified potential new customer sectors, gave fresh views of the customer value scheme, and proved push for moving the

---

[33] Kaplan, Robert, and David Norton. "Building a Strategy-Focused Organization". Ivey Business Journal. June 1, 2001. Accessed August 21, 2014.

transformation and the corporation forward. By 1996, Rockwater was first in its forte in both growth and profitability.

Chase Bank. Chase Bank began using the BSC in 1993 to help the bank integrate an acquisition, to bring together more integrated financial services, and to hasten the use of electronic banking. The BSC clearly defined the strategic primacies and delivered a structure to tie strategy and budgeting together. In a span of only three years, profitability increased twenty fold.

These four cases demonstrate the clout of the BSC approach. These executive teams positively executed their strategies when the majority of their contemporaries could not. But the speed with which the results were realized focuses the potential that exists for every organization. The abilities for success were already present in these organizations. These organizations achieved their incredible results with the same team members, the same resources, and mostly the same products and services. The team members already had the knowledge and skills needed to execute the decisions and strategies. They only lacked the comprehension, the concentration, and the orientation of where the organization wanted to go. The BSC removed these barriers and provided the emphasis that unlocked the strategic knowledge and skills of the organization.

Organizations that effectively implement scorecards reinvent each moving part of their organizational structure to have an emphasis upon strategy. This is a major departure from customary management programs that tie performance to financial structure such as budgets and value approaches. The successful organizations create a performance-management system that puts strategy at the epicenter of its management processes. Continuing research has shown a set of five principles that allow organizations to develop a strategy-focus enabling the organizations to execute their strategies quickly and efficiently.

Five Principles of a Strategy-Focused Organization

1. MOBILIZE CHANGE THROUGH EXECUTIVE LEADERSHIP
- MOBILIZATION
- GOVERNANCE PROCESS
- STRATEGIC MANAGEMENT

2. TRANSLATE STRATEGY INTO OPERATING TERMS
- STRATEGY MAPS
- BALANCED SCORECARDS

BALANCED SCORECARD

5. MAKE FORMULATING STRATEGY A CONTINUAL PROCESS
- LINK BUDGETS & STRATEGY
- STRATEGIC LEARNING
- ANALYTICS & INFORMATION SYSTEMS

3. ALIGN ORGANIZATION WITH STRATEGY
- CORPORATE ROLE
- BUSINESS UNIT SYNERGIES
- SUPPORT UNIT SYNERGIES

4. MAKE STRATEGY EVERYONE'S JOB
- STRATEGIC AWARENESS
- PERSONAL SCORECARD
- BALANCED PAYCHEQUES

FIRST: MOBILIZE CHANGE THROUGH EXECUTIVE LEADERSHIP

A positive BSC program begins with the acknowledgment that it's not a "metrics" project, but a "change" project. The single, most imperative condition for achievement is the ownership and dynamic participation of the executive team. Strategy changes entail modification from every portion of the organization. If those at the top are not enthusiastic leaders of the process, change will not occur and the opportunity will be lost.

John Kotter defines how transformational change must originate at the top, with three discrete behaviors by the leaders. The leaders of successful BSC implementation followed this model[34]:

- **Create a sense of urgency.** Before change can happen, the organization must be "unfrozen" in order comprehend why dramatic change is required. In the case studies outlined above, the organizations were undergoing challenging and very difficult situations. However, the need for change which was very obvious to executives at the top was not always obvious to the remainder of the organization. Team members were content with the status quo. They needed a stimulus to assent that change was required and inevitable if they were produce the benefits of a new organizational focus on strategy. The initial step in the change process for each of these organizations was to communicate the need for the change.

- **Develop the leadership team.** The dynamics of the executive leadership team frequently determines whether the BSC idea works or not. The leaders of effective BSC organizations recognize that their present collection of functional experts have to be changed into an integrated team that is strategically focused and cross-functional. Members of executive teams often have a habit of viewing management concerns from their individual, functional viewpoints. These executives usually have surprisingly little cognizance of how other functions within work. Successful adopters of the BSC supplement their customary executive team with managers who are experts on the identified strategic issues. When moving or reemphasizing wider customer bases, a marketing specialist may be needed. When products change, technical expertise may be needed in the boardroom. The adding of new perspectives is indispensable in breaching the traditional obstacles to teamwork that sometimes exists at the top.

- **Develop the Vision and Strategy.** The establishment of a common vision and strategy is a valuable way to construct an executive leadership team. An effective executive leadership team is not simply a collection of divisional or departmental managers that occasionally meet together to discuss organizational issues. The outline of the BSC guides the

---

[34] John Kotter, Leading Change, Harvard Business School Press, 1996.

leadership team in its developing a new vision and strategy. A tremendous amount of interaction takes place as each component of the new strategy is adapted to the organization's score card design. Strategic issues concerning customer segments and marketing, yield optimization and manufacturing, cost of capital and finance, and supply-chain management, transportation and warehousing become the shared concerns of the executive leadership team. Historically, each of these issues was deemed to be the dominion of a single functional executive. However, in the strategy focused organization that is no longer true.

SECOND: MAKING STRATEGY WORK

Positioning strategy at the center of the management system suggests that strategy can be defined so that it can be comprehended and acted upon. Regrettably, there are no criterions for strategy. If we are going to build management systems around strategies, we need an authority for describing strategy that is both trustworthy and stable.

The Balanced Scorecard approach provides that authority for the successful organization. As well as building scorecards, the process helps executive teams to better fathom and to better express their strategies. The base of the design is a Strategy Map, which outlines the "architecture" of the strategy.

The top section of the map addresses the financial perspective. After all, the ultimate goal of most organizations is to make money. Improving shareholder value holds the top spot of this top section as the ultimate indicator of success. Other long-term and short-term indicators of financial success are also placed in this section.

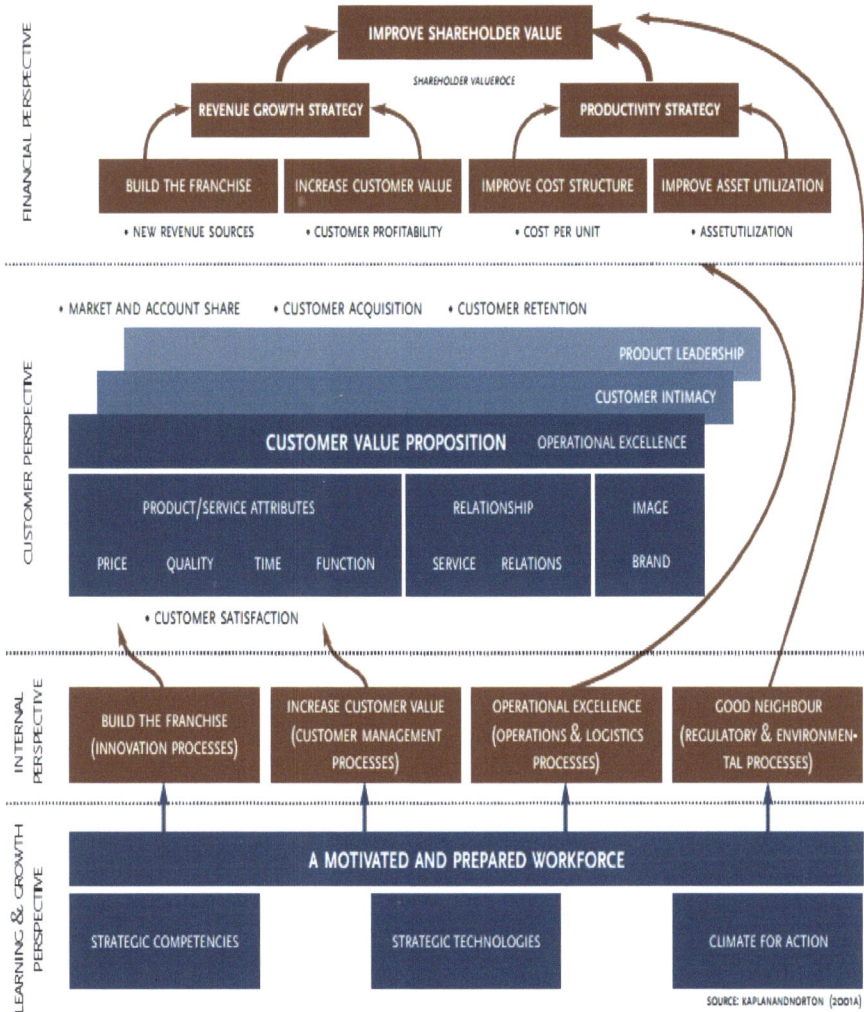

FIGURE 2: THE BALANCED SCORECARD STRATEGY MAP

SOURCE: KAPLANANDNORTON (2001A)

The map continues downward with the customer perspective being the second section. Profitability depends upon customers purchasing the product. This section identifies and places measurable indicators of customer response and product performance. Various targeted customer segments are differentiated so that varying strategies for reaching the different customer segments can be established and measured. And from those individual indicators an overall measurement can be defined.

The third section is the internal perspective. This section places the internal indicators of success on the map. Indicators of supply chain efficiency, regulation compliance, taking care of customers, and innovation are located here. Again, these indicators should be measureable.

The bottom section of the map is the learning and growth perspective. This section indicates the competencies, technologies and climate essential to support the distinct requirements of the customer value proposition and the internal processes.

This Strategy Map also links the various indicators of the different perspectives and indicators above. Regulatory compliance has a direct bearing upon improving shareholder value. Operational efficiency is a base factor in forming the financial perspective. Internal innovation directly effects product development and customer satisfaction.

After the Strategy Map has been outlined and settled on by the executive team, creating a scorecard that measures and targets is a less complicated process. The Strategy Map approach underscores that Balanced Scorecards should not be a collection of financial and non-financial measures that happen to be organized into four perspectives. A Balanced Scorecard should reveal the strategy of the organization. A good test of an effective Strategy Map and Balanced Scorecard is to look only at the map and the scorecard. Do you understand the strategy that is attempting to be measured?

Scorecards and strategy maps should be logical and comprehensive. They should visually describe the organization's strategy. They should distinctly indicate the desired outcomes and the in-place strategy for achieving those desired outcomes.

THIRD: ALIGNING THE ORGANIZATION WITH THE STRATEGY

The BSC is a potent tool to define an organization's strategy. However, organizations are made up of many business subunits, departments, teams, and specialized sectors. Each of these individual sectors has its own operations, its own goals, and local strategies to meet those goals. In order for the overall organizational strategy to work and the overall goals to be achieved there must be collaboration. For collaboration to occur, the strategies throughout these units should be synchronized. The BSC can and should be applied to define the strategic relationships that integrate the performance of multiple units into the primary organizational strategy. However, this is not an uncomplicated task. Functional units and departments, such as marketing, finance, sales, purchasing, manufacturing, and engineering, possess their own distinct reservoirs of knowledge. Isolated functional storehouses can arise and then become major obstacles to strategy implementation as most organizations have major trouble communicating, collaborating, and harmonizing across such varied functions. For organizational performance to be increase beyond the simple sum of its parts, these individual unit strategies need be allied and combined. The executive leadership team and its immediate subordinate teams have the primary role in defining these links and ensuring that collaboration is actually occurring.

The top organizational strategic positions guide the creation of the Balanced Scorecards for the individual units and sectors. Each unit formulates a strategy suitable for its target indicator in light of the specific conditions and situations that are organic to its operations (i.e. competitors, market opportunities, operational processes). This or these new or revised strategies are consistent with the positions and priorities of the overall organization. However, without continued impetus from upper leadership levels, this strategy formulation and collaboration is not likely to happen quickly or with much real thought. People who are content do not readily embrace change. Therefore, the Corporate Scorecard (the overall organizational scorecard) should provide the mechanism indicating and measuring the needed communication and collaboration across the individual unit scorecards. The individual subunit managers and leaders will

60

choose the local measures and strategies that are best suited for achieving that unit's contribution to meeting the organizational goals. While some subunits' measures translate easily from the subunit to the higher organizational levels (i.e. finance), other units' measures do not directly aggregate into the top-level measures (i.e. community service/involvement and Human Resources).

Beyond aligning the business units, strategy-focused organizations must also align their personnel functions and common supporting units, such as HR, information technology, facilities management, finance, and purchasing. In BSC organizations, frequently this alignment is completed with a working service arrangement between each functional supporting unit and the business subunits. The service arrangement states what services are to be provided by the supporting unit, including their functionality, the expected level of quality and the cost for the support. This service arrangement becomes the base of the Balanced Scorecard constructed by the functional supporting unit. The supporting unit's customers are the internal business subunits. The value of the support the supporting unit provides is defined in the service arrangement. The financial objectives are derived from the budget for the supporting unit. Next, the supporting unit ascertains the internal processes, and the learning and growth objectives that drive its internal customer objectives and financial objectives.

Once this process is complete, all the organizational units should have definite, precise strategies that are expressed and measured by strategy maps and Balanced Scorecards. As the subunit local strategies are integrated, they strengthen each other. This alignment allows collaboration to occur so that the whole is greater than the simple sum of the parts. Relationships can also be established across corporate boundaries. Organizations can construct BSCs to outline their interactions with key suppliers, individual customers, vendors, and joint ventures. These scorecards are useful to explicitly and overtly indicate to the external party the objectives of the relationship, and how the performance and contribution of each party in the relationship is measured by factors other than simple cost and price.

FOURTH: MAKING STRATEGY EVERY TEAM MEMBER'S RESPONSIBILITY

According to academic and governmental sources, it is estimated that around 50 percent of all work accomplished in industrialized countries in the present day is knowledge work. Workforce knowledge is an asset that we are only now beginning to use efficiently. In a strategy-focused organizational structure, strategic information and decision-making in no longer restricted to executives and senior managers and leaders. Knowledge workers render strategic choices each day. Successful BSC users take steps to make sure that all organizational team members understand the strategies, are aligned with them, and are capable of executing the understood strategies. Human resource systems and processes play a vital role in aiding this transition through in the following ways:[35]

- **Communication and learning to create awareness.** A requirement for executing strategy is that all employees comprehend the strategy. A constant and permanent communication program is foundational for organizational alignment. No single vehicle is sufficient to ensure every team members' understanding of the strategy. It must be transmitted in all communication media and vehicles and underpinned by the personal behavior of executives.
- **Personal alignment.** Successful BSC users align team members with the strategies via personal goal-setting processes. Some organizations even create personal scorecards for key team members. Individual measures and strategies created within the outline of the BSC are cross-functional and longer-term.
- **Incentive compensation.** When BSC is successful, organizations should quickly move to link an incentive reward to targeted scorecard measures. This link unleashes increased motivational forces. Modifying behavior, which is the goal of a strategy-focused organization, is not an easy thing

---

[35] Ibid. Kaplan, 2001.

within established organizations. Reward for doing so is merited. Linking the incentive reward program to the BSC measures increases voluntary team interest in the strategies' details.

FIFTH: MAKING STRATEGY FORMULATION A CONTINUAL ORGANIZATIONAL PROCESS

Organizations usually form their management processes around their budgets and their operating tactics. They conduct regular team and management meetings in order to appraise performance compared against the plans. Variances from previous performances are discussed. Negative short-term variances are noted and new action plans for dealing with these undesirable variances are requested. Tactical management, such as this, is necessary, but, unfortunately, this is the only strategic management that management often does. Other than the annual strategic planning meeting or retreat, usually there are no other meetings where team leadership meets to formulate strategies.

What is the problem with this? Remember the battlefield general? Environments, situations, conditions, and circumstances are in a continual flux. A great tactic today will probably not work tomorrow due to the varying conditions that affect operations. Thus, strategies need to be continually in review and undergoing readjustment. Organizations that implement the BSC take on a new "double-loop process" to accomplish strategy. This process incorporates the management of tactics with the management of strategy. This is accomplished by using three key processes:[36]

First, organizations connect strategy to the budgeting process. The organizations use the Balanced Scorecard as a monitor for assessing possible investments and initiatives. The operating budgets of most organizations manages the required spending for producing the organization's products and services, and the

---

[36] Ibid.

marketing and selling of those products and services to existing customers. By focusing strategies and using the BSC as a measure, organizations now initiate a strategy budget that funds initiatives that will cultivate entirely new abilities, spread to new customers and markets, and make drastic improvements in current processes and abilities. This distinction between current operating funding and funding for future growth in the budget is crucial. The Balanced Scorecard tries to protect long-term objectives from short-term devices. Likewise, the budgeting process needs to shield long-term initiatives from the pressures to supply short-term financial performance.

The second step in making strategy formulation a continual process is to initiate regular team leadership and management meetings to appraise strategy. This is an obvious sounding step, but a step that does not happen in most organizations. Under the BSC format, such meetings happen at least monthly to discuss the scorecard. Attending these meetings are managers from across the organization. These managers are there to monitor organizational performance against the organization's scorecard short-term target goals. They are looking to find out if the financial and non-financial goals and measures are being met. They are also verifying that strategic initiatives are being executed as planned. While similar to the commonplace monthly operating reviews, these strategic meetings not only review performance and take needed tactical corrective action, the leaders and managers review feedback from the subordinate teams and units. Optimally, this feedback will already provide strategic observations and suggestions. And since this feedback is already aligned with overall organizational strategy, these new or adjusted strategies are even now ready to be implemented.

Information response systems will need to change to support the new strategy meetings. Organizations may want to create an open reporting atmosphere in which performance results are open to all team members in the organization for review. This builds upon the notion that strategy is the responsibility of all team members. Team members feel more engaged and are more empowered by this knowledge so that they can do their jobs better. An open reporting atmosphere may also cause unexpected payoffs as innovative and proactive team members may come up with new tactics and strategies to address shortcomings or may identify new ideas and opportunities to exploit successes. The open sharing of strategic information assists in producing an organizational culture that may truly revolutionize an organization's former hierarchical approaches to information and power.

The third step required for making strategy formulation a continual process is the recognition that learning and adapting and changing strategies is never ending. The initial Balanced Scorecard exemplifies a hypothesis about the strategy. This hypothesis, though based upon reason, logic, experience, and some measures, has still yet to be tried. This initial scorecard and hypothesis is the best appraisal of the suggested actions that are expected to create a long-term financial success. Designing the scorecard establishes an explicit connection between cause-and-effect in the suggested strategies and the results. As the scorecard is put into effect and the feedback system begins reporting the actual results, the organization is able to test the hypothetical strategies. And then through the testing of the hypothetical strategies, strategic doctrine can be established.

But more importantly, what happens in these meetings is the recognizing and realization that modifying and formulating of strategies is continual. A fresh type of energy is created. Team members use words like "fun" and "exciting" to describe these strategy meetings. One senior executive stated that the monthly strategy meetings became so popular in his organization that "there was standing room only and he could have sold tickets to them."[37]

Organizations should also utilize the strategy meetings to seek and to pursue new strategic opportunities that are not currently on their scorecard. Events can transpire that were not projected at the time the strategy and scorecard were designed. Ideas and learning develop continually from inside the organization. Rather than waiting for next year's annual meeting, priorities, strategies, and the scorecards are revised immediately. The executives and team leaders of successful organizations use the ideas and learning created by their organization to perfect their strategies. Instead of being an annual event, the forming of strategy, its testing, and the revision of strategies become a never-ending process.

---

[37] Ibid.

The Balanced Scorecard has allowed organizations to introduce a new control and appraisal process, one that is focused on strategy rather than tactics. This new control process stresses learning, team problem-solving and coaching. Strategic review meetings now consider the future, discovering how to execute strategy more efficiently, and recognizing the changes that need to be effected in the strategy – founded on what has been gathered from the present application of the strategies.

This is a management process adjusted to the needs of today's businesses. The necessary ingredient is a simple structure and tool that permits strategy to be conveyed clearly. Without such a strategic structure, there can be no strategic management system. The Balanced Scorecard is the core of the management system that strategy-focused organizations use to shape their future.

High-Performance Organizations

Very quickly after walking into a high-performance organization, you begin to feel a difference. Rather than just going through the motions of doing assignments, you feel that the people around you are real team members. They are energized. They are secure about what they are doing, and they know why they are doing what they are doing. Ask them about their organization's strategy and they will speak of the strategies as if they just came from the board room. They know what changes are happening and why they are needed. They know how their tasks relate to other team members and in the overall organizational process. Your initial observations are quickly confirmed by reviewing performance measures and scorecards.

But how do organizations develop into high-performance organizations? We all know instinctively that it is the organization's resources and the abilities of its team members that drive operational and financial performance. It is these combined capabilities that allow organizations to implement their strategies. But the problem is that most organizations do not measure these organizational capabilities. They do not know how. And even fewer organizations know the steps to follow to improve these capabilities. Senior and executive leadership possess excellent tools to monitor operational and financial performance, but not for driving the organization's and its people's capabilities

This gap needs to be filled-in with effective tools. To begin filling this gap we need to recognize the most common organizational and people characteristics of high-performance organizations. Fourteen such characteristics have been identified that lead to sustained performance. They can be placed into five broad categories:[38]

---

[38] Bhalla, Vikham, and Jean-Michel Caye. *High-Performance Organizations*. Boston, MA: Boston Consulting Group, 2011.

- **Leadership.** An allied leadership that is effective when entrenched deeply within an organization.
- **Design.** A lean organizational framework that manifests the organization's strategic focus and has well-defined roles and responsibilities.
- **People.** The organization efficiently translates business strategy into a potent people strategy which appeals to and retains the most capable team members.
- **Change Management.** The organization has the capacity to propel and maintain organizational –wide change and to foresee and adapt within progressively more volatile environments.
- **Culture and Engagement.** The organization's culture is fashioned to accomplish strategic goals, and its employees are inspired to go further than what their tasks require; the employees are just as motivated to achieve overall organizational objectives as individual goals.

In order to generate long-lasting increases in performance and to establish a competitive edge, organizations should mold their strategic approaches is such a manner that these five broad categories and the fourteen characteristics within these groups are monitored and improved upon.

Leadership

High performance teams of individuals drive urgency and direction
The pipeline is stocked with future leaders whose skills are matched to future needs
Middle managers embrace and translate strategy

Design

Structure and resource allocation reflect strategic tradeoffs
Few layers separate the CEO and the frontline, and spans of control are wide
Accountabilities, decision rights, and collaboration are constructed with thoughtful consideration

People

The employer brand is a core asset
Critical roles and key talents are clearly identified and treated with care
HR is a strategic partner and an enabler of the business

Change management

Change is a deliberate force
The organization is evolutionary

Culture and engagement

Culture accelerates strategic objectives
Engagement is measured and cultivated to generate discretionary effort from employees

[39]

---

[39] Ibid.

Leadership

Leadership is an uncommon resource, both in developed markets, where there is a current exodus of senior executives, and developing markets that are laboring to keep up with the swift growth. Today's quicker pace of change has deteriorated leadership that is conducted exclusively through command and control. An efficient leader reasons strategically, sets the tempo, allocates resources, encourages engagement, urges accountability, and produces results. This is not a set of tasks that is easily accomplished in good times, much less in ambiguous times. Leadership begins, but does not end, at the top of the organizational structure. High-performance organizations produce leaders at all levels through three primary mechanisms.

In high-performing organizations, it is team leaders that display urgency and provide the direction of that urgency. The leaders are comfortable with intricacy, unpredictability, and change. Though often facing uncertainty

Wal-Mart Leadership

In the early 1980s, this author, while living and working in Arkansas, owned a small business that supported insurance companies. This business allowed for me to meet and talk with many business, government, and civic leaders – the rich and famous you might say. One of those leaders that I met was David Glass, an early CEO of Wal-Mart. Mr. Glass related to me that one of his and Sam Walton's ideas for staffing management positions in the Wal-Mart corporation was to fill a third of the positions from internal promotions, to fill a third of the positions with top candidates from the competition, and to fill a third of the positions with talent that were recent graduates or came from areas and industries that were not directly related to the retail industry. Their reasoning was that the internal group knew the company and would keep things on track. The group from competing retailers would bring in ideas that were already working. The non-retail group would bring completely new ideas and would be willing to try anything new. It is apparent that their staffing ideology worked for them.

as change occurs, the leaders are able to mobilize team members to the current tasks.   Though leaders must to be visionary, they cannot be independent operators or lone wolves; the days of the single, heroic leader that saves all is over. Today's leaders must collaborate, cooperate and utilize the cooperative strength that occurs through team work. Increasingly, leaders have to be at ease in dealing with parties from outside the organization such as government regulators, supporting organizations and other external bodies that are now more active in the daily activities of business.

High-performing organizations have maturing leaders that have already been identified and are being prepared for future positions. These team leaders have worked in several types of roles, positions, functions and are prepared succeed. High-performance organizations spot potential leaders early on in their careers and then nurture into those leaders the skills and capabilities that will be essential in the future. Studies show that low performance companies fill top leadership roles with only 13% of internal candidates.   Whereas, high-performance companies fill 60% of those top roles from promotions of their existing team members.[40]

Mid-level leaders and managers in high-performing organizations support and render strategy. These team leaders direct the vast majority of an organization's team members. It is their interpreting the strategy and ideas that are favored by senior leadership into the workable tactics for their teams. These team leaders are also the ones that identify and bump-up the vital issues from the organization's frontline that require senior leadership's attention. In spite of the central and difficult function that mid-level leaders have, they many times are forgotten, do not receive adequate development opportunities, are not supported, and get too little attention from senior leadership. High-performance organizations recognize the value of these important team leaders.   These organizations invest in the success of middle management leadership and work to increase their technical capabilities as well as their people management skills.

---

[40] Ibid.

Design

Good organizational design can aid companies to improve their executing and achieving strategic goals. However, in order for that to happen, there must be back-and-forth between the key elements of structure, capabilities, task roles, and collaboration. This is where the design comes in. The organizational design of high-performance organizations coordinate and closely link the overall strategy with the subordinate strategies and tactics giving them a competitive advantage.

In the high-performing organizations, the design of the structure and the organization's resource allocation reveal strategic tradeoffs. Compromise is integral in organizational design.

Role charters are not simple job descriptions. Team members participate in the composing of their role charters. The charters focus on accountabilities and decision making, without detailing activities. Role charters are not static; rather they should be revisited and revised regularly to reflect changing strategic and tactical priorities.

A well-designed structure emphasizes what is most important to an organization *and* in the real world we cannot accommodate all facets of an organization equally. For example, a company that is focused on growing future key markets may want to organize business units by region instead of by product channels. Hence, company leadership would need to make sure that product channels (i.e. research & development, production) receive proper support though do not form the primary axis in the organization. High-performance organizational structure is dynamic and is oriented toward current and future priorities. As strategies, performances or other business and competitive conditions change, the organization's structure will may need readjustment.

There are as few layers as possible separating senior leadership and the frontline team members in a high-performance organization. Therefore, spans of control are broad. Lean structures allow organizations to focus on important, significant work rather than being preoccupied on vertical coordination. Those activities that do not deliver value are jettisoned. Due to fewer organizational layers, decision-making, communication, and feedback occur more quickly and organizational response happens more rapidly. Senior leadership has a better idea of what is happening in day-to-day operations and customer interactions. The broader spans of controls require managers and leaders to be more ambitious and creative in utilizing their leadership and people skills. These managers and leaders do not have the time to micromanage. This forces them to become comfortable in their leadership abilities, requires them to become coaches and mentors, and requires them to be encouragers. Team leaders are also forced to be more selective in team staffing.

When designing structure in high-performing organizations, considerable thought must be given to accountability, who makes the decisions, and who collaborates on decisions. High-performance organizations have unmistakably distinct roles that are wisely accumulated to form a well-organized organization. (Having written *Role Charters* greatly assist in articulating team member roles.) Team members understand what is anticipated of them and which decisions they are to collaborate with and which ones they are to make. The sharing of accountability promotes the understanding of who will be collaborating, when it will occur, what will be collaborated, and who will make the final decision once the collaboration has happened. Having these well-defined roles and decision paths removes any ambiguity that hinders the decision-making process. This role and path definition also improves team member potential performance and their engagement within the organization. These defined roles facilitate honest conversation between team member peers and between team members and their leadership concerning individual, cooperative, and communal responsibilities.

Matching the right team member with the right capabilities is essential to achieving maximum operating performance. Depending upon the current needs, an organization's sales team might need a team leader that is an excellent "closer" in order to invigorate the team. At another time, it might need a strong manager that can better apply a new sales strategy. But unless the wider needs of the organization are explicitly communicated, managers and leader may hire and promote team members based upon their personal perception of a "good fit".

When staffing positions, organizational leaders and managers should consider whether a role requires an excellent change agent or a technical expert or a steady pair of hands. High-performance organization's make sure that there is a balance of these different type leaders across the organization. The organization recognizes that roles will change, thus so will the need for these leaders with these capabilities. As the needs of a role changes, often times the person filling that role will need to change. While this pragmatism may sound harsh, it, in reality, is beneficial to the organization as well as the individual team member. Sitting leaders and managers that have been given a tasking for which they may not have the best or adequate skill set needed to accomplish the task will have increased stress and other less than positive reactions. A lateral shift or the bringing in of a co-leader or assistant may well keep performance levels high as well as helping to retain a valuable team member.

People

Many organizations are strong at recruiting and training (also called performance management); however, high-performing organizations are extremely efficient at turning their business strategy into an enthralling and forceful people strategy. In these high-performing organizations, HR and people management departments functions as a strong advisor to the business units on operational and strategic people concerns. Effective people management departments have not only short-term plans for current staffing needs but also makes plans and projections for long-term staffing. The people management team is continuously determining how to identify, to attract, to develop, and to retain the right team members with the right capabilities; further, the people management team is anticipating changes in organizational strategy and changing people needs. High-performance organizations have a distinct employer trademark. Think Google, Zappos, and Southwest Airlines. Team members and candidates both know of the wide range of benefits – beyond direct compensation – that team members enjoy. These benefits include career advancement, quality of work life, rotating through other positions and tasks, prestige, job contentment, autonomy, and flexibility. This organizational branding adds to an organization's overall strengths and increases its competitive edge.

High-performance organizations capitalize upon employee development by providing training and learning opportunities and by revolving people through different roles, tasking, and responsibilities. These different experiences are a potent motivational and retention instrument that can supersede direct compensation and other monetary incentives. Moving through various roles and positons will also boost collaboration while reducing the likelihood of insulated leadership behavior. Upon reaching the upper levels of leadership, the team leaders have a wide and comprehensive panorama of the organization.

However, there is always the flip side of people management. No matter how careful, skillful, and diligent an organization hires, there will usually be a few unpredictable mishaps as to the candidates hired. And individuals do change as circumstances in their personal lives change. People management includes taking care of poor performers. The manner in which an organization deals with developing low-performing team members and the removing of chronic low-performers sends a very strong message to the rest of the team members as to what will be tolerated, what is unacceptable, and what will be celebrated.

The critical leadership roles and the highly talented, highly valuable team members that fill those roles are identified early and treated appropriately. But while doing this, high-performance organizations are deliberate in letting it be known why they consider these roles and those filling those roles as valuable. This deliberate communication does not have to be loud and overt. Rather, subtle comments and indirect ways of indicating this importance is probably the most effective of dissemination of this type information. Publishing and celebrating performance success and the value of that success is one way. Open role charters and telling what that role entails and how and why a team member is excelling in that role is another. The more other team members know why and how someone is valuable to the overall team, the more the other team members will embrace the talented individual. And doing so may have the added benefit of motivating others to mimic the talented and valuable member's behavior.

But talent management is even wider than simply taking care of the very talented. It should not be reserved solely for those fast-track team members. Most team members are not on the fast-track and many critical roles will not be filled by fast-tracked team members. Those individuals with special people skills (i.e. "closers" on sales teams and relationship managers in banks) and those with highly technical skills (i.e. laboratory technologists and IT specialists), though they may never hold a major leadership role, need to be regarded as the valuable talent that they are. High-performance organizations also recognize these crucial roles and the uniquely talented individuals that fill those roles. People management concentrates and customizes retention strategies and contingency tactics around those particular team members.   This list of these team members and roles should be dynamic as it will change with the firm's changing strategies.

People management is a strategic collaborator and an "enabler" in the high-performance organization. People strategy is as important as business strategy and should be given equal priority.

Change Management

The business environs in our world today are fast-paced and becoming even faster moving with each new technology and the constantly changing market climates. These new and changing technologies have direct impact not only on the internal processes, strategies, and technologies of organizations but also on the external influences. Three major external influences that are in constant flux today are:

- our customer's needs and desires;
- what our competition is doing,
- and socio/political/economic conditions.

Those organizations that are able to quickly respond to the three volatile external influencers affecting them will enjoy a competitive advantage. In order to respond quickly and realize the competitive advantage organizations must be able to change themselves in two very fundamental ways. First, the organization has to have a methodical approach to shifts in organizational emphasis, strategy, course, structure, and thought processes. Second, the organizations must have the ability to recognize the quickly developing trends in the market and have the willingness to adapt and change to those trends.

Change is a disciplined force. Many organizations fail and fall under the weight of change. High-performing organizations have learned to beat the odds against them when change needs to happen. They do this by beginning with leadership. These organizations make sure that leadership is aligned and in agreement with the goals of the change. Leadership has collaborated with the means to effect the change. The organization consciously and methodically transfers this alignment to its team members from one lay and to another downward and outward throughout the organization. Higher leadership receive feedback from those team members located deep within the organization and from the frontline members that are in direct contact with customers. This feedback is scrutinized so that progress of the change and reactions to the change can be monitored. Adjustments to the change process can be made based upon these measured responses. By maintaining their focus on the primary and most vital elements of forced change, an organization is able to achieve minimum sufficiency. Minimum sufficiency is doing just enough with just enough resources to achieve the desired change without unnecessarily splitting focus and effort and unnecessarily expending resources. Minimum sufficiency happens by utilizing hard and soft strategies to effect the needed change. Accountabilities and measures are defined for individual team members. The team members are given the tools and the authority to successfully implement the change required at their position and tasking. As the change is happening, the organization tracks the progress of the change against the previously identified milestones. Thus, the organization is quickly aware if and when change initiatives are possibly at risk in falling behind schedule or failing in certain areas or at certain levels. The organization can then take needed corrective action. The organization also establishes open communication and engages key stakeholders, internal and external, during the change. This engagement permits customers and supply chain elements to possibly offer assistance to the organization, to understand and be prepared for effects to their processes with the organization, and instill greater confidence in the organization due to this transparency. The approach of minimum sufficiency has proven to be a primary key in the financial success of high-performance organizations. A high-performance organization is evolutionary. They are adaptable, continually perceiving changes in the market and effecting strategic adjustments.

An international pharmaceutical company recently used a deliberate, disciplined change to realize more than a $1 billion earnings increase in confronting large legal, regulatory, and competitive challenges. The restructuring of the organization required the complete commitment and involvement of leadership from the senior executive team though the organization to the manufacturing level.

One executive-committee team member handed over the larger part of his daily executive responsibilities to subordinate leaders allowing him to devote more than half of his time to directing, coordinating, and monitoring the forced change. The remaining executive team members shared time and efforts as leaders in cross-functional teams that carried out change strategies. The senior leaders employed "belief audits" and "experience mapping" and other change tools to discover points of agreement, points of misunderstanding, and areas of misalignment.

The teams delayed initiating projects until alignment existed in all the collaborating teams. Team contracts and role charters coupled with program management techniques created transparency and were used to measure results. The discipline required for the alignment, goal achievement, and progress monitoring spread quickly and smoothly throughout the organization as it was leadership that not only led but was also very actively involved in change execution.

This methodology is supplemental rather than substituting when changing the broad strokes of the organization's strategy. The organization empowers the teams and team members on the peripheries of the organization to immediately initiate responses to anticipated market developments rather than waiting to react after market conditions have already changed. At the fast-pace of today's world, reacting after the fact results in always playing catch-up rather than leading.

Organizational Culture and Team Engagement

Organizational culture is the manner in which things get done in an organization. This overall culture mirrors team members' behaviors, approaches, mindsets, and attitudes toward work. It is the non-tangible component of an organization that can bring down an organization in spite of endless tangible resources. Just as military history as shown that the biggest and best equipped armies can be brought down without soldiers that have a fighting, courageous spirit, so can fall the largest of organizations. Organizational culture is not static. It should be living and manageable. It is possible and necessary to nurture and to develop a desired, specific culture. Team member engagement is the enthusiasm of employees to go a bit farther for the good of the organization than is required to simply accomplish a task. They do this extra service not

Recently two European banks merged. These two banks had very different business structures and organizational cultures. One bank was extremely skilled in selling products directly to customers. The other had success traditional branch banking setting. The success of the merger was dependent upon the integration of the two cultures.

First senior leadership had to agree upon the vital, desired key behaviors first needed to agree on the key desired behaviors of the new organization as well as the behaviors' uniformity with stated core values. The bank's top three leadership levels met regularly in order to be sure that the various levels were in alignment and to monitor the forward progress of the makeover. In order to move these desired behaviors beyond the upper management levels, the bank customized training to the unique challenges found at each level of the organization. Tool kits were developed to assist in the conveyance of each core value.

To be very sure that the changes would be cemented into the desired culture, the bank established behavioral expectations into team and individual performance reports and reviews. Since the merger began, the new bank has monitored team engagement and customer retention. The scores in both of these areas have been very high. The new bank is ahead of its predicted milestone in financial and new customer targets.

out of mere obligation or for their paycheck; they do the extra because the organization and the success of the organization is important to them on a personal level and on the professional level.

Culture and team engagement are not the same as leadership, design, people, and change management. Rather, culture and team engagement result from possessing the other twelve characteristics from those four groups. High-performing organizations enrich and develop culture and engagement subtly and tacitly by cultivating and developing the other characteristics in the same manner people indirectly exercise their hearts by directly exercising their legs and other body muscles. Performance management systems, for example, are an element of the people dimension. A performance management system that rewards performance without punishing well-thought-out, well-executed, good ideas that happen to fail will stimulate motivation. This motivation will have a very potent effect on the organization's culture.

Organizational culture can hasten the execution of strategic objectives. A positive organizational culture does not happen by accident. High-performing organizations establish, manage, observe and monitor internal culture in order to better accomplish strategic objectives. An organizational culture that highlights risk aversion, proven processes before implementation, and absolute individual lines of command and responsibility may not only be reasonable but also required for an airline. However, this culture will only bring failure to an Internet technology company. A culture will either work for an organization at a specific time or it will not. As strategies and priorities are adjusted and changed, organizational cultures should also be induced to change.

Team engagement is gauged and cultivated to create discretionary endeavor from team members. At a high level, this engagement is fostered through two equally imperative dimensions:

- personal motivating factors, such as recognition, and
- performance disciplines, such as performance management metrics.

High performing organizations constantly monitor their team members' morale, attitudes, and desire to add to the organizational value through difficult periods of time such as major change, reorganizations, and business downturns.

Most commonly, organizations react with knee-jerk responses to external events. These organizations will add staff in good times, cut staff during slack periods, and mandate leadership training when the inevitable diminished morale shows up. These organizations then suffer with the whiplash reaction and the unintended consequences of these sudden and not-well thought out responses.

Others organizations take a laissez-faire tactic. They take no deliberate initiatives to engage team members and simply allow events to play out even to the long-term detriment of people assets. Neither the knee-jerk reactions nor the laissez-faire tactic has positive influences on performance.

High-performance organizations simply work differently. High-performing organizations comprehend the necessity of having all fourteen characteristics firmly established within their organizations. These high-performing organizations take an active, coordinated methodology to implement, formulate and develop these characteristics. They decide which of the fourteen are most critical to their organization's maintaining a competitive advantage. These organizations deliberately work to build up and improve the weak areas with a meticulous, well-ordered, educated array of interventions and movements. The following exhibit outlines common interventions that high performing organizations employ.[41]

---

[41] Ibid.

The Best Ways to Stay on Track

Leadership

Measure the impact of leadership appointments and intervene accordingly
Optimize the time and energy spent on an increasing variety of stakeholders
Establish a forward-looking leadership profile for recruitment purposes

Design

Increase spans of control and reduce layers and the size of management ranks
Realign the organization structure with strategic priorities and make appropriate tradeoffs
Redevelop the role of middle managers to drive impact and engagement

People

Assess future talent needs and align recruiting with them
Redesign the employer brand to resonate with employees and recruits and differentiate from competitors
Refresh the people development strategy to include divisional and regional rotations for

Change management

Build mechanisms to track the impact of corporate initiatives and anticipate when they might be at risk
Develop a disciplined implementation process that assigns individual accountability
Empower leaders and middle managers, according them the flexibility to anticipate and

Culture and engagement

Define the desired culture required to enable strategy
Refine recruiting criteria to ensure that cultural aspirations are clearly reflected
Assign horizontal accountabilities to drive cross-enterprise collaboration and engagement
Identify groups with missing or inappropriate career paths and make adjustments to drive

High performance organizations watchfully monitor and evaluate acquiesce of its team members to the characteristics that the organizational leadership has identified as crucial and decisive for the sustained competitive advantage that the organization needs and desires to succeed. Markers and measures attesting to the achieving of these characteristics are seen to be as just important measures for success as financial and operational performance markers.

The quest of the correct characteristics – organizational and people related characteristics – need not be a trial and error search.

Role Charters

Organizations are becoming increasingly global in span and reach. This wider scope is creating the need for more complex structures within organizations. However, in these increasingly more multifaceted, multipart organizations, decisions and questions which need to be made and answered are often times left unresolved and unanswered. Team members that should be collaborating are, instead, warily circling one another – hesitant and perhaps even with distrust.[42]

Role charters are a tool that can aid in removing hesitancy and distrust within teams and organizations. The role charters make sure that essential decision-making and collaboration for decisions happens between team members. These charters are simple devices that facilitate those sometimes difficult and tense conversations between leaders and between team leaders and their teams. Inevitably, tensions will surface in within teams and organizations – that is simple human nature. And the ever-increasing complexity found within the matrix of ever-farther-reaching organizations creates greater confusion and tension. These organizations with their cumulative demand for collaboration across the organization and from external customers, find that their teams and team members are often times answering to more than one "boss". It is the perceived notion that a team member must please two "bosses" that creates major job stress in team members. And rather than relieving the tension, traditional Human Resource processes will often exacerbate the tension.

A role charter makes clear what team members are accountable for certain tasks, what team members are contributors to the decision-making, and who the final decision lies with. The charter also establishes behavioral expectancies and measurements to be sure that success in carrying out the tasking and making the decision is happening in the most efficient, identified manner.

---

[42] Killmann, Julie, Micheal Shanahan, and Andrew Toma. *Role Charters*. Boston, MA: Boston Consulting Group, 2011.

Going Beyond Job Descriptions

Role charters are not simple job descriptions even though role charters do contain role descriptions and responsibilities that may be similar to the HR job descriptions.   HR job descriptions reflect the existing roles and responsibilities of a particular position. However, these descriptions are not directly coupled to the organization's vision, objectives, and measures. But role charters are so coupled. Role charters are dynamic documents that are designed to be permeated with organizational strategy, day-by-day work objectives, and the overall objectives of the organization's teams and individual team members. Role charters define roles as they ought to be. The charters also detail the required collaboration among various roles so that assigned tasks can happen.

Designing and agreeing upon role charters generally occurs during a reorganization, restructuring, or transformation. These events can be at a local team level or involving the entire organization. Developing role charters should be an integral element when designing an organization's structure and formulating its culture. Creating role charters can also be an effective tool to promote new opportunities for growth, for infusing new leadership behaviors, and for enabling other essential realignments. Creating role charters can revive these initiatives if resolve is weakening, execution of strategy or tactics have slowed, or if resolving conflicts in priorities remain a problem.

Another significant difference between role charters and job descriptions is how the role charters are written. Job descriptions are usually produced with no participation of the team members who will be holding the position. The positions' leaders or managers makes the description based solely upon their personal interpretation – accurate or inaccurate – of how the positions' tasks should be completed and what KSAs are required for completing the tasks. Role charters, however, are created by the team members that will be holding those positions. The team members coordinate and collaborate with the team leaders and their peers to assure that the charters are functional in the team and organizational setting.

DESIGNING ROLE CHARTERS

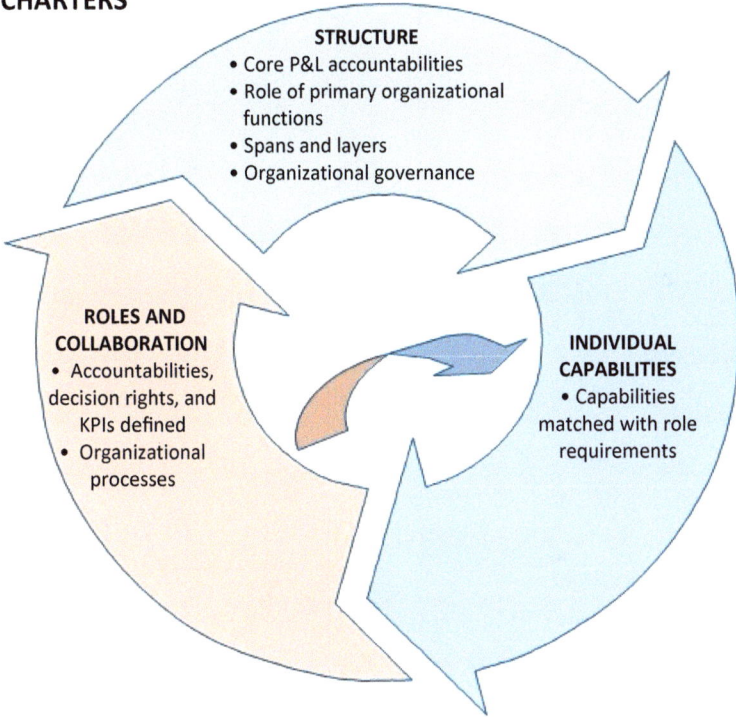

STRUCTURE
- Core P&L accountabilities
- Role of primary organizational functions
- Spans and layers
- Organizational governance

INDIVIDUAL CAPABILITIES
- Capabilities matched with role requirements

ROLES AND COLLABORATION
- Accountabilities, decision rights, and KPIs defined
- Organizational processes

Designing Role Charters

A role charter's potential lies in its design. The process of developing a role charter requires higher leadership and collaborating teams to become involved, to accept, and to commit to the charter and the position by fostering the group comprehension of the charter and position.

To begin the process a CEO or business unit or division head renders the overall organizational into five correlated elements of his or her role:[43]

- Accountabilities which are essential to the success of the organization and those accountabilities for which only he or she is responsible
- Accountabilities which are essential and but shared with other leadership
- Key performance indicators (KPIs) which are used to gauge the execution of the identified accountabilities

- The decision rights that he or she needs to execute the

Designed for Performance

Organizational design can and should offer an efficient and practical solution to many persistent strategy and business-execution issues. If a redesign is to be successful, senior leadership must recognize that all three components of design — structure, individual capabilities, and roles and collaboration — are critical in making the change.

If thinking of an organization's structure as its skeleton; we see individual capabilities as its muscular system. These muscles provide the working force and strength. Roles and collaboration becomes the nervous system which gives direction to the muscles.

Even the very best design will fold or collapse if the correct people with the right skill sets are not in the right jobs. And even having the right people in the right jobs is not a guarantee against failing if the roles are indistinct, overextended, or confusing. Role charters can help combine all three pieces of an organization into a design customized for high-performance.

---

[43] Ibid.

individual and shared accountabilities
- Leadership behaviors considered essential for the success of the organization

These accountabilities, measures, decision rights, and behaviors function as the "role charter" for that senior leader. That leader then meets with all of the subordinate team leaders that report directly to him or her. In these meetings, the charter and the overall organizational objectives are discussed. These subordinate team leaders then write their own charters. This is an important step in the process as it is the persons holding those positions that best know their role and how to do it as well as how their individual roles will invariably overlap with leaders in other roles.

Simply glancing at a template for a role charter, it may appear as merely a page of rectangles in which team members write in their individual and shared accountabilities, how their job performance can be measured and judged, and the decisions that they influence, can make, or can overrule. However, there is great value in the information in those rectangles so long as the correct process is utilized in filling the rectangles. When correctly executed, this process forces team leaders and their charges to ponder accountability, performance measurements, decision rights and behavior all together in a single conversation. This group consideration of these elements exposes concerns and problems that may slow decision-making and hinder collaboration, but at the same time defining team expectations. Another benefit of the group consideration is the linking of roles to improved organizational performance.

After all subordinate team leaders have finished their charter, the senior team leader convenes a workshop where all of the leaders present their individual charters. This is a workshop and not a typical business meeting. This workshop is an open session in which the senior leaders as well as all in attendance are free to speak and to address the problems associated with each of their roles. It is natural for vagueness, disagreements, and confusion to occur in any dynamic organization's structure. This workshop is the place for these issues to surface and to be addressed. This is the place in which tensions between senior leaders and peers and other team leaders can be resolved. That being said, ***it is only if*** *the senior team leaders and all those present have a positive, humble, cooperative attitude that maximum positive results will actually be realized.*

The workshop should be run by a facilitator and not a participating leader. The facilitator should be skilled in conducting this type of workshop and also have superior people skills in reading and engaging people. The success or failure of the workshop hinges greatly on the enthusiasm and staunchness of the leaders taking the role chartering process and their personal charters seriously. If the senior leader directing the process treats the process as a significant exercise, so will the subordinate team leaders.

Individual accountabilities		Parameters for success	
Each individual's critical responsibilities, such as delivering quality products		Key metrics	Organizational parameters
		Critical performance indicators, such as market share, aligned with the organization's vision and goals	Organizational, governance, and legal structures, such as direct or dotted-line reporting relationships or decision ownership
		Financial targets	
		Critical financial indicators, such as revenues or direct cost management	
Key collaboration network/collaboration			
Key shared accountabilities	Mission-critical collaborators	Decision rights	
Critical account-abilities shared with another member of the management team	Employees with whom this individual must collaborate in order to execute shared accountabilities	Owns	Influences
Key shared accountabilities	Mission-critical collaborators	Decisions for which the individual is directly responsible, such as the product launch schedule and product budget	Decisions in which the individual's opinion counts, such as sales strategy and pricing decisions
Key leadership behaviors		Vetoes	
Behaviors the leadership team seeks to embrace, such as improved collaboration		Decisions that the individual does not control but has authority to approve or veto	

When the workshop concludes, all the team leaders and members participating should have a completed role charter for their positon. This completed charter should also fit together with the other participant's charters. Each role charter expounds upon the team member's individual accountabilities as well as the measures that will be used to gauge performance in these accountabilities and responsibilities. The charter will also outline expected associated leadership behaviors. As for shared responsibilities, the charters resolve define who the "owner" of the final decision is, which team members influence the decision, and which team member can veto the decision. The role charters indicate not only what responsibilities are shared but who is responsible for resolving the task and decision.

Once the upper leadership has agreed upon their individual charters, the process is repeated with each descending or lateral team leader; each leader propels the charter creation throughout his or her subordinate team leaders. The senior leader provides higher-level objectives to their subordinate team leaders on which those subordinate leaders base their individual charters. Each group or level holds its own workshop to complete each participating leaders' charter. This process continues throughout the targeted organizational leadership.

The process of creating role charters at each level typically takes a couple of week to complete. Of course this depends upon the quickness of the team members to write the initial charters and the timing of the workshop. Depending upon the nature of the organizational makeover or restructuring involved, role chartering is usually limited to the upper two or three layers of the organization or unit. And role charters are dynamic. They should be reviewed at least annually or when a significant shift in roles, alignment, or authority has occurred.

The role chartering process is valuable because the process produces alignment on accountabilities from the top leadership of the organization to the mid and lower leadership. The process is structured, progressing level-by-level. This places all leaders on the same page. Since all the participating leaders have had their input in the role chartering, each of them has a personal stake in making sure that the makeover or restructuring succeeds. Personally discovered insight is always more valued than when conveyed by someone else.

The Keys to Successful Role Charters

There are a few clear-cut practices that can help to make sure that the process of developing role charters is beneficial and persistent and not just another trend that is forgotten in a short while.

- **Horizontal Conversations, Vertical Implementation.** Team members are comfortable in communicating with their leaders and managers. Leaders are comfortable in talking with their team members and in working with their teams. However, the horizontal conversations, the communicating with peers at their level is less common; especially when the communication involves honest discussion of how things get done in the organization and how they should get done. Peers are often reluctant to declare who has the final decision and who only influences the decision. It is the creating of the role charter that forces these difficult discussions to happen across teams and even across organizational boundaries. Creating role charters in the explained structured manner encourages honest discourse and will bring personal or hidden agendas into the open.

  The optimal way in which to employ role charters is through the level-by-level cascade as described above. Using this method makes certain that senior leadership is aligned and they are transferring that alignment to their leadership positions below them. As the cascade continues, team leaders at all the levels will have roles that have distinct, appointed authority to make decisions thus engaging those leaders to become invested in the outcome of their decisions.

- **Action Plans with Buy-In.** Role charters reveal real-world tradeoffs that are necessary within organizations in ways that job descriptions cannot. They are derived from actions that the working leadership realizes should be happening. The leadership has bought-in with these recognized, needed actions by their taking part in forming their own charters. These leaders have had input in what their roles are, in what their responsibilities are, how they should be leading, and how their performance will be measured. Nothing is new to them and nothing is being forced on them without their being able to address these expectations. The leaders realize that if their charters are not realistic, they will be ones paying the price. Thus, it is in their best interest to become very actively involved in creating their charters.

- **Fewer Is Better.** Role charters should not attempt to be an extensive list of all possible accountabilities and measures for a particular role. Instead role charters should concentrate on the most important ones. The chartering process, from top to bottom, is similar to a funnel with a filter on its bottom opening. Discussions and charters and the discussed accountabilities, measures, and decision-making roles at each level enter the wide opening of the process funnel and passing out the bottom, through a filter of cooperative discernment, exits what matters most at this level. In most senior level leadership charters, the senior leader owns four to five critical decisions. That senior leader has influence in another two to four decision-making areas, with veto authority in an additional two to four decision areas. That senior leader's charter lists an average of four accountabilities. In traditional business structures, this may seem like a limited scope of influence. However, studies have revealed that when encumbered with too many areas of influence, the senior leader is unable to execute that influence.[44] Similarly, when accountability is shared among many executives and leaders, it becomes easier to point fingers when problems arise rather than resolving the issues.

By concentrating on the accountabilities, measures, decision rights, and behaviors which matter most, well-designed role charters provide team members well-defined guidance as to their responsibilities, how they are expected to behave, and how they are to be evaluated and rewarded.

---

[44] Ibid.

All of these things, including the ambiguous issues, have been discussed in the workshops, agreed upon, and then written down.

- **Shared Decision-Making.** In most modern organizations, the sharing of responsibility is increasing. Most critical decisions demand input from various team members and usually more than one senior leader has a major role in the decision. These senior leaders are often located in different areas of the organization and oriented toward different disciplines and organizational functions. This shared decision-making is even more pervasive in the increasingly common matrix-structured organizations. In organizations where shared decision-making is an integral part of the culture and structure, role charters are of even greater value in establishing decision rights and accountabilities

- **It Begins at the Top.** The Role chartering process should begin at the top of the organization. Senior leadership and team leaders are organizational role models. If the senior leadership is not committed to the reorganization or makeover of the organization, the team members will quickly detect this ambivalence and only intensify it. To expect team members to collaborate and work across organizational boundaries if their leadership cannot or will not is completely unrealistic.

However, role chartering is not to cease at the top. As beneficial as it is to have all the senior leaders working from same conceptual framework, the greatest potential from role chartering happens as the chartering occurs deeper into the organization. It is the various new approaches of working together that team members discover in the workshops that the greatest benefit is derived. While it may be impractical to realize role charters to include each and every team member, the process should include the minimum of three or four management levels and through the key team leaders' positions. Without this minimum involvement reaching deep into the organization, long-lasting and meaningful change is unlikely to happen.

Though great tools, role charters are not panaceas for every ailment of a struggling organization. Nor are role charters a magic potion that will bring success to every organization. Role charters are not the only tool needed to repair an inefficient organizational structure. And role charters do not inject those knowledge and skills into an organizational workforce that it does not already possess. However, role charters are a very potent lever that can assist in maneuvering an organization into a high-performing organization.

Quality of Work Life and Team Members

Though defined in 1989, it was not until 1997 that business academics first proposed that quality of work life was a driving factor in high-performing, growing, and profitable organizations.[45, 46] Since that time, it has become proven through studies that healthy team member relations are definitely a key to an organization's success.

In order to promote healthy employee relations, an organization must have clearly described guidelines and procedures for people management in order to prevent confusion, issues, ambiguities, and to recruit and retain talent. If an organization simply reacts to problems when they happen, inevitable losses to an organization's tangible and talent resource pool will also happen. Increasing competition, multifarious economic environments, mounting labor costs, and other factors require organizations to take up proactive employee relations strategies. Organizations have to assure the realization of organizational goals and strategies through the cooperation and engagement of its team members. The composition of organizational teams continually changes. As a result of this continuing change in team make-up, those organizations that focus on quality of work life (QWL) of its team members will have a growing leverage in recruiting and retaining talent.

QWL is a wide-ranging agenda designed to improve team members' gratification in their being part of an organization and working in the organization. QWL is an approach to thinking about people, their work, and their relationship with the organization. QWL can create a feeling of accomplishment in the minds of the

---

[45] Robbins, S.P. (1989), *Organizational Behavior: Concepts, Controversies, and Applications*, Prentice-Hall, Englewood Cliffs, NJ.

[46] Heskett, J.L.; Sasser, W.E. Jr. and Schlesinger, L.A. (1997), *The Service Profit Chain*, The Free Press, New York.

team members and can promote greater job satisfaction, which, in turn, enhances productivity, flexibility, proactivity, and overall success of an organization. QWL agendas and programs emphasize amiable employee relations and adopt a human resource strategy which places a very high value on viewing team members as organizational stakeholders. Additionally, organizations with ardent employee relations programs will profit from a highly motivated team workforce that desires to give maximum effort for an organization that treats them fairly, consistently, and that values them.

QWL Initiatives as Employee Relations

In order to understand how QWL initiatives function as an integral part of employee relations, we need to understand more fully the totality of what employee relations encompasses. A descriptive definition of employee relations is:

"'Employee relations' is a common title for the industrial relations function within personnel management and is also sometimes used as an alternative label for the academic field of industrial relations. The term underlines the fact that industrial relations is not confined to the study of trade unions but embraces the broad pattern of employee management, including systems of direct communication and employee involvement that target the individual worker."[47]

"Employee Relations involves the body of work concerned with maintaining employer-employee relationships that contribute to satisfactory productivity, motivation, and morale. Essentially, Employee Relations is concerned with preventing and resolving problems involving individuals that which arise out of or affect work situations."[48]

---

[47] Heery, E. & Noon, M. (2001). *A dictionary of human relations*. Oxford: Oxford University Press.

[48] NASA's Goddard Space Flight Center Office of Human Relations. (2001).

With this understanding and comprehension of employee relations, it is now much easier to see how QWL initiatives are so potent in bringing positive value to those high-performing organizations that choose to embrace them.

The academic definition of QWL is "a process by which an organization responds to employee needs by developing mechanisms to allow them to share fully in making the decisions that design their lives at work".[49] QWL is recognized as a multi-dimensional model with various concepts, some of which may not be universally standardized. Rather, some of these particular concepts may depend upon cultural and societal norms of the organization's workforce. The basic concepts described and discussed in the HR and business academic literature consist of job security, improved reward systems, increased compensation, career development, team member engagement. We are able to develop a working definition of QWL as the positive conditions and atmospheres of a workplace which sustain and encourage employee satisfaction through the provision of job security, opportunities for advancement, and rewards.

A key facet of QWL is a continual effort to increase the cooperation between the organizational workforce and its leaders. This cooperation is centered on solving organizational problems and improving team member job satisfaction; satisfaction which directly bears on organizational performance, and thus, also directly affecting the team members. Team members have a positive role in QWL initiatives by promoting, sustaining, and even defining what QWL is for them. Team members can indicate that QWL is a legitimate instrument that represents the group's perceived rights and interests. Team members, as a group and as individuals, that collaborate and communicate with the organization their ideas and notions of what they feel QWL is, feel more engaged with the organization. This engagement also minimizes confrontation and realizes desired changes in QWL.

What is employee relations? Retrieved on November 15, 2005, from
http://ohr.gsfc.nasa.gov/employee_relations/whatis.htm.
[49] Ibid. Robbins.

Mutual respect is the basis of the overall QWL movement and its conceptualization. It is only in an atmosphere in which the team members and the organizational leadership and the "organization" demonstrate respect for each other that QWL can work to maximum benefit for all parties.

Bringing QWL into the Organization

While the above academic definition of QWL is excellent for our academic studies, most of us need a bit more practical way of thinking about QWL. Let's try this one:

> *"QWL is the degree to which members of a work organization are able to satisfy important personal needs through their experiences in the organization".* [50]

In the practical application of QWL we see a process. The process is includes the organization and its team members. Ideally all of the team members, team leaders from all levels, and those executives that represent the whole of the organization collaborate in order to form the organization's environments, its methods, and the outcomes of how it operates. This value-based process is intended to meet the two goals of superior organizational effectiveness and an improved quality of life in the workplace for the team members. Quality of work life endeavors are systematic efforts made by the organization to provide its team members greater opportunities to influence the way they do their jobs and tasks and in how they contribute to the overall success of their organization.

Quality of work life is often references eight comprehensive conditions and criteria of employment which create a desired QWL. These same criteria can be used for measuring team members perceived QWL. These conditions and criteria include:

- Adequate and fair compensation,

---

[50] Though this definition has been widely attributed to a "J. Richard and J. Loy" this author was unable to find the original reference or use of this definition.

- Safe and healthy working condition,
- Opportunities to use and develop personal capacities,
- Opportunity for career growth,
- Social integration in the work force,
- Having definable rights as a member of the organization,
- Work and quality of life, and
- Special relevance of work.[51]

Working is fundamental part of our daily life. It is our source of revenue, our career, how we often identify ourselves. Working is what we do with about one-third of our entire life. Work and our workplace have a major influence in the overall quality of our lives. Ideally, our work at the end of each day, should provide us with contentment in what we are doing, we should have peace of mind in what we are doing, and have a sense of fulfillment for having completed a meaningful, fruitful task. Though the day's work may have only been a very small step in reaching our life's goal, we should have satisfaction enough to look forward to the following day. It is when an organization's team members have this sense of satisfaction that the organization is on its way to becoming a high-performance organization.

---

[51] Walton RE, 1973. Quality of work life: what is it? *Sloan Management Review Journal*, 15, 11-21.

Leading Change

Way back in the day, the senior leadership of large organizations had a simple goal for their organizations and themselves. That goal was stability. Corporate shareholders asked for little more than predictable earnings growth. Since most markets were undeveloped or closed, the corporate leaders were able to provide for those expectations. It took little more than annual strategy meetings from which only token alterations to the established strategic plan were made. Costs remained within projections. Employees remained in their jobs. All was good.

However, in the past decade, transformation and organizational change management have grown to be undeviating facets of the business landscape. Countless new markets desiring the newest products, vast and different labor sources, raw material availability, political climates, and pioneering technologies have made many of the once-powerful business models unrewarding. The need for capital liquidity, liquidity to enable an organization to work through and to take advantage of these changes, has been magnified. Meeting these challenges has created more sophisticated practices that high-performing organizations employ to manage change. These change-prepared organizations are extremely sensitive to and acutely aware of the role that organizational culture plays in facilitating change. These organizations are also very good at following though so that the forthcoming next change is even smoother.

Experiences in organizational change management within high-performing organizations indicate that there are three primary obstacles that must be overcome to facilitate change.[52]

What should be no surprise is "change fatigue". Change fatigue is the exhaustion which people feel when they are compelled to make too many modifications at once. This fatigue often occurs as the result of change initiatives that were poorly

---

[52] Aguire, DeAnne, and Micah Alpern. 10 Principles of Leading Change Management. *Strategy Business*. June 6, 2014. Accessed August 28, 2014.

planned, executed too quickly, or started without proper preparation. While change has to happen and can happen effectively, the bringing about of complex change requires multiple smaller steps. Change fatigue is also a familiar problem in organizations whose executive leadership pushes through trendy changes that that have no real benefit upon the majority of the organization's team members. High-performing organizations avoid change for the sake of change. Rather a business case is built for each change and the value of the change is carefully evaluated before a decision to implement the change is ever mulled over.

Change initiatives also falter and fail due to an organization lack of skills to make sure that the change can be maintained over time. Organizational leaders are invariably eager set out to bolster product quality; however, when the resources began to look sparse and production slows, these leaders will often lose heart. Having production problems that they do not have a ready solution for, the leaders often blame production technology or conclude that their targets were too optimistic. Or worse, the leaders accuse their frontline team members of not being suitable for the task. A far better resolution to the problem is to do some investing in the initiative. Operational improvements in the way of innovating and redesigning processes and training in the new processes and anticipating potential hurdles with an already considered contingency plan will keep change initiatives moving in a positive direction. These are also the practical approaches which provide team members with the knowledge and cultural support they need to embrace the change.

The third major impediment is that change initiatives are usually decided upon, schemed, designed and instigated in and from the highest levels of leadership and usually with little input from the team members at the lower levels. This lack of lower team level involvement keeps information which might be useful in designing the initiative from being added to the change plans while also restricting opportunities to give ownership of the change to the whole of the organization.

Ten Principles for Guiding Successful Change

1. **Let culture lead.** Lou Gerstner, the CEO that led IBM through one of the most successful business makeovers in history, stated that the most valuable lesson he learned was that "culture is everything".[53] Leaders of high-performing organizations understand this. Various business academic surveys indicate that the overwhelming most critical factor in change management is to address the organizational culture. Yet change leaders continually neglect to focus on culture. These non-engaging leaders neither attempt to overcome cultural resistance (in a productive manner) nor do they utilize any cultural support that they may have. These change leaders fail to sustain the change nearly 80% of the time.

    Why is this fact of failure true if all of these leaders recognize and understand the critical nature of culture during a change? It has been offered that change leaders view the organization's culture as a past legacy that needs to be left in the past. However, it must be remembered that the team members that will be executing the changes are the human beings whom have strong emotional connection to the present culture. Change managers can become so involved in the structural details, formal processes, decision rights, and accountabilities that they forget human nature. These change managers presume that because culture is lenient and informal it is also malleable enough to adjust on its own without needing overt attention.

    But it is the skilled change managers whom are mindful of best practices to organizational change who continuously utilize their organization's culture to successfully bring change. Rather than attempting to modify the culture itself, they derive emotional vigor from it. They use how team members already think, how they work, behave, and feel to deliver a lift to the change initiative. In using this emotional vigor, leaders look for the components of the culture that are in alignment with the change,

---

[53] Ibid.

bringing these components to the forefront, which attracts the attention of those team members that will be affected by the change.

Skilled change managers whom are mindful of best practices to organizational change continuously utilize their organization's culture to successfully bring change.

Two healthcare companies were undergoing a merger. The change managers wanted to allow culture to lead the integration. A culture-related questionnaire was designed. The questionnaire asked team members to express each company's operating style. The change managers graphed the responses to have an idea the combined strengths and weaknesses of the two different companies. Quickly it became evident that one of the companies focused on bottom-line results while the other company focused on process. The new company, in order to have the greatest success, would need to use processes as its primary strategy. It was the taking the time to identify and to acknowledge to the underlying culture of the two different companies that the leaders of the new company discovered the key strategy for success to the new company. It was also by learning that the bottom-line approach was generic to the one group of employees, that the change leaders discovered how to approach those employees in order to begin the change initiatives.

2. **Start at the top and move downward.** While it's essential to engage team members at every level early in the change planning, all fruitful change management initiatives begin at the top. It is an unswerving and well-aligned group of senior leaders that is clearly supported by the CEO or owners from which successful change initiates. This alignment cannot be viewed as optional. Effort has to be made in advance to make certain

that everyone is in agreement with why the change is needed and the details for executing the change.

Several years ago a clinical research firm committed itself to triple its size in ten years. The company wanted to leverage itself into a more competitive position. As the company was still operating like a startup company even after 25 years, a major organizational makeover was required. Early on, before the design phrase even began, the financial leaders of the company held a conference away from the company's facilities. This conference was a painstaking exercise in bringing alignment to all leadership. The exercise began with a survey to determine effectiveness of the leadership team. This survey revealed that although these leaders termed themselves a team, they really did not view themselves as a team. Rather the majority of them operated independently of others, as lone rangers. This is a characteristic of startup organizations.

Each executive in the group gave a thorough, individual presentation speaking to the case for the impending change. The greater part of the group was in agreement upon the general direction that the company should take to achieve the desired rapid growth. However, the descriptions of the initial strategies and tactics on how to move in the agreed upon direction were wide and varied. The group was then instructed to work together in developing a business case for change that each of them could support.

This tasking required each of these top executive to listen attentively to their collaborators and to consider differing points of view. The exercise was taxing, but the group began to unite around a reasonable vision of what the organization should look like in ten years. More importantly, the experience of collaborating in such an intense manner caused the executives, for the first time, to act as a combined and committed team. At the end of the conference, the group was using the same language and had a common vision. The coming together of the top leadership allowed the change initiative to cascade to other groups at lower levels of the hierarchy.

3. **Involve every level.** Change managers will often fail to consider the influence that midlevel and frontline team members have in the success or failure of a change initiative. The process for rolling out change is infinitely smoother if these mid and lower level members are engaged early for input on the change issues that will be affecting their tasks and positions. Frontline team members are apt to be rich sources of knowledge about where probable hitches may occur. They know what technical and logistical concerns need to be dealt with and they know how customers will probably react to the changes. Additionally, with their engagement and whole-hearted support, a much smoother execution for more complex change initiatives is probable. However, resistance by these middle and lower level team leaders and team members will make execution an unending challenge.

Change managers may not engage early-on the multiple levels of the organization because they feel that the fewer people involved in the process the better efficiency. But this idea flies in the face of human nature: change is easier to accept when ones peers are accepting the change. Though it may take more time and effort in the beginning, the assuring of broad engagement will save countless headaches later. Broader engagement not only allows for more to surface, but more team members are invested when the have a hand in developing the plan. Change management exemplifies the common dictum "you have to go slow to go fast."

In 2003, when IBM began to roll their organizational culture change initiative, they recognized the need for the engaging of the mid and lower level team leaders and members. The leadership teams had met extensively in order to develop clear-cut definitions of the cultural traits the company needed to go forward. After these meetings, the change management team then established a website in which any team member was able to post concerns, comments, suggestions, and responses. The website was active for three days. After the three days, the change managers were then able to make key modifications on the input they received. It was also clearly communicated that the input received from the whole of the organization was being incorporated into the change initiative.

4. **Be rational but let emotions assist.** Senior team leaders and executives will often promote a major organizational change solely based on strategic business goals such as "15% per year growth for the next three years" or "we will break into new and emerging markets". Such goals and objectives are fine so far as goals and objectives. However, objectives presented simply as business goal, will rarely connect with team members in an emotional way. It is emotional connection that brings genuine commitment of team members to a cause for change. Humans react to calls for actions that not only engage their minds but also their hearts. Humans want to feel as if they are a part of something bigger than they are.

    In 2013, Hewlett-Packard's CEO, Meg Whitman, and her executive leadership team began using this principle in that company's makeover endeavors. Seeking to trigger strong personal connections between the company and its team members, the executive leadership team began drawing directly on the organization's cultural history and its traditions. The fences that separated the executive parking lot were torn down. Many of the top leadership were moved into cubicles. Though symbolic, these gestures reminded people of and reinforced the "HP Way" ethic that valued intrinsic work quality of a team member as much as a team member's position in the company hierarchy. Interestingly, this strategy stands out against the strategies of Whitman's immediate predecessors. The three CEOs prior to her had pronounced that it was time for HP to abandon its core identity. HP's stock has steadily increased since Whitman's team began their organizational makeover. In any organization confronting a challenging situation, the emotional connection fostered by practical and symbolic moves will likely make a profound difference.

5. **New thinking requires new actions.** A lot of change initiatives are formulated under the assumption that team members will modify their behaviors and actions as soon as the directives and incentives have been announced. Some leaders believe that collaboration across functional teams will automatically begin when new lines are drawn on the organizational chart. It is thought that managers will begin to communicate better because they have a message of a new strategy and a mandate to deliver that message.

But lines on the organizational chart and confident declarations of intent have only so much power. Extremely more critical to the realization of any change initiative is assuring that people's daily actions and behaviors reveal the imperative of change. Begin by outlining a few critical behaviors that are essential to the accomplishment of the initiative. Then go about everyday business with those behaviors in the forefront and center. Senior leadership need to visibly demonstrate these new behaviors themselves from day one. Team members will only believe that real change is happening if they see it occurring at the top of the organization.

6. **Engage, engage, and engage some more.** Leadership will often make the error of thinking that if they put into words a forceful enough message of change at the beginning of an initiative, team members will comprehend what to do. But nothing can be farther from the truth. Forceful and continued change must have constant communication. This communication must not end after the initial rollout but to continue well after the major pieces of the plan are in place and operating. The more varied and different ways that the plan's elements are communicated, the more effective the communication is. HP's tearing down the fences and moving leadership into cubicles were effective communication methods. Symbols underline and strengthen the impact of words.

7. **Outside the lines leadership.** The best opportunity for successful change moving through an organization happens when all the team members with influence and authority is involved. Besides the organization's

recognized leaders, there are those team members whose potency in the organizations is less formal. These maybe those team members who have specific expertise or skill in key task areas, have wide connections within their organizational network, or have those personality characteristics that engender and generate trust. These informal leaders are found throughout organizations. They may include a highly regarded and skilled field manager, an innovative project director, or an office manager who's been at the firm for ten years. High-performing organizations succeed at implementing major change by identifying these informal leaders early and find ways to engage them to participate and to guide the change. There are three distinct kinds of informal leaders:

- There are pride builders. These are those team members who are great at inspiring and motivating others to take pride in what they are doing. They inspire other team members by making people feel good in working for the organization and to have a desire to go beyond that which is simply required.
- There are the go-to team members. These are the people who really know how things happen inside of an organization. Team members seek out these go-to people when something needs to be done immediately and with minimal problems and questions.
- There are change or culture ambassadors. These team members know, almost instinctively, how to carry out the change that is coming down. These people can be shining examples as well as excellent communicators in relating to other team members why the change is vital.

Informal change agents must be identified before they can be enlisted and engaged. In large organizations, a network analysis is the best way to accomplish this. Through mapping out connections and finding out who people talk to, change managers are able to determine the informal spheres of influence that are outside the organizational chart lines.

8. **Leverage formal solutions.**   Change managers may persuade team members to embrace the change and modify their, however, unless the formal organizational elements of operating procedures, structure, team development and training, and reward systems, are redesigned and modified to promote the desired changed behavior, the change will stop dead in its track. Often times change managers will organize committees or teams to help in the bringing about the desired change. However, for a myriad of reasons, these committees do not receive the tools they need, the authority to do what needs to be done, nor any form of reward for taking on the additional tasks. No one can be expected to work long in such an unsupported tasking.

9. **Leverage informal solutions.** Though the formal elements that are required to support the change are present, an established culture can hinder and even stop a change process if team members revert back to the long-held, unconscious mindsets. Informal solutions can work well with formal solutions.

    A few years ago, a major computer-technology manufacturing company was attempting remake its culture into one that was more customer-oriented after a decade of cost-cutting emphasis. Countless surveys showed major customer disappointment with the company's products. The company was selling poor-quality, flawed products.   New procedures, quality control measures, and front-line team structure were implemented.

    However, one of the most potent of the change solutions was entirely cultural and informal. For ten years the informal motto of the frontline teams had been, "ship it no matter what". That slogan was changed to "if it is not right, do not ship it!" Informal and formal organizational leaders were engaged to implant that message into everyone so that flawed products would no longer be shipped and sold. Even if it meant disassembling products to check the quality of components, then it had to be done. Stopping or slowing down production would just have to occur if necessary to ship only good products. By requesting team members at every level to be responsible for quality and giving every team member the authority to stop a bad product from leaving the assembly facilities a new ethic of organizational ownership was formed.

10. **Evaluate and adapt.** A 2013 survey exposed that many organizations involved in makeover, transformation, and restructuring efforts fail to measure their accomplishment before moving forward.[54] Change team and organizational leaders are so ready to claim victory that they do not take the time to find out what things are not working. This failure in follow-through creates inconsistency and denies the organization of needed information in how to support the change process throughout the remaining parts of the change cycle.

A very large, international consumer products company had committed to lowering production costs. Organizational leaders constructed a full-bodied change template and executed it across the organization. Evaluation metrics indicated that the change initiative was succeeding. However, the company sought to be sure that people comprehended the continuing nature of this lower production cost commitment. The change management team instituted a series of quick, short surveys and assembled focus groups to describe the case for the change and the new actions and behaviors needed of everyone.

The initial round of surveys showed that only 60% of those answering the survey understood the message. The change management team then began engaging informal leaders to play a bigger role in communicating and supporting the initiative. The surveys and focus groups continued to measure the progression of the change comprehension until a more sizable majority of the team members showed that they understood that the change was long-term.

---

[54] Aguire, DeAnne, Rutger Von Post, and Micah Alpern. *Cultures Role in Enabling Organizational Change*. San Francisco, California: Booz & Company, 2013.

111

These ten guiding principles present a potent template for team leaders that are committed to realizing sustained transformational change within their organizations. The work required to bring a successful makeover and change can be arduous and exacting. However, the demand for major change initiatives is only going to become more urgent and more powerful. High-performing organizations will get the change process done right.

Constructing a Business Case for a Change Initiative

Let's begin with what a business case for a change initiative is. A business case describes the logic and the reasoning and the deciding for why a project or task should be initiated and presents this debate in a manner to influence a decision maker to take action. In constructing a business case for a change initiative, there are four key questions to answer:

What *exactly* is the project or task? The business case recommends a *specific* project or task. Note the emphasis on *exactly* and *specific*. Be precise in what should be accomplished and why. The project or task is to join a planned change management approach to a particular initiative or project.

What is the reason for the task or change? The business case communicates the logic, the reason and the rationales for introducing the project or task to the organization. For a change management business case, the thinking is that the ultimate, bottom-line benefits, the values that are created, and the achieving of desired outcomes and results are directly connected to managing the people aspect of change.

Who are we attempting to convince? The audience of the business case is those decision makers who will ultimately take the actions in funding, supporting, and leading the project, task, or initiative. For a change management business case, the probable audience will be senior leadership and team leaders and managers.

What is the action we need to happen for the project or task to succeed? The business case is most often utilized to acquire funding and commitment for the project, task, or initiative. The action needed for a change initiative business case is 1) a commitment from the decision maker to employ change management as part of the project or initiative and 2) the authority, the resources, and the funding to utilize change management.

While the business case is a common tool when relating to projects and tasking initiatives, the same tool, can readily be used to translate and to construct a formal business case for change management.

Sections of the Business Case[55]

A business case explains the entire story of a proposed project or task. To be complete, it is advisable to use the eight section business case format and then apply the format to a business case for change management. Those eight sections are:

1. **Executive Summary.** Neat and concise presentation of critical information. It condenses your story. For change management your story is that we are commencing a most important project and this project has a significant "people side" element. The proposition is to employ change management as strategy of the project in order that the desired and intended project outcomes and results and outcomes are accomplished.

2. **Situational Assessment and Problem Statement.** Precisely connects the benefits, values, outcomes, and results of the initiative or project to the people side of the change. This section does not exactly reference change management, rather this section outlines and describes dependencies.

3. **Project Description.** Communicates the high-level description, breadth, objectives and goals for the project or initiative. In this case the initiative or task is the application of change management. Through absolutely defining the task of applying change management, you are showing the

---

[55] "Why a Business Case for Change Management." Business Case for Change Management. June 1, 2013. Accessed August 31, 2014.

decision maker confidence that can and will address the presented situation effectively.

4. **Solution Description.** Condenses your solution of applying change management. Describes indicators, work flow, and evaluation metrics for change management. Utilizing objects and terms familiar to project leaders (i.e. indicators, milestones, and work flow) displays the objectivity of change management and makes it less fuzzy.

5. **Cost-Benefit Analysis.** Distinctly presents the costs and projected benefits of applying change management. This section is concentrated on the final outcomes and results of the completed project and the benefit of applying change management to the project and what could happen if change management is not applied.

6. **Implementation Timeline:** Establishes a structured tactic and maps the change management milestones.

7. **Critical Assumptions and Risk Assessment.** Renders a SWOT Analysis and describes the dependencies for applying change management.

8. **Conclusions and Recommendations.** Plainly articulates the needed items (resources, funding, authorization, support, etc.) in order to successfully bring about the change initiative from start-up through follow-up. This section relates with confidence that you solution solves the situation presented in this business case.

Addressing the Challenges and Objections of Change Management with a Business Case

A business case portrays what it actually means to employ change management on a project

The Project Description section and the Solution Description section of a business case for change management depicts, in absolute and tangible terms, what happens when change management is applied to a project including an overall description, breadth, goals, work flow, milestones.

A business case states the value of change management

The Situational Assessment and Problem Statement sections of the business case for change management precisely link the results and outcomes of the project to the management of the people aspect of change. This section, in not even directly mentioning change management, illustrates the realizing of values and benefits as dependent on the ultimate embracing and practice of the solution by affected employees.

A business case reveals the thoroughness and resoluteness of change management

The utilization of a business case in and of itself indicates that change management is a real and solid element of organizational management. In presenting an approach and reasoning from the people aspect of change in a formal business case, credibility and the insistence of change management as vital to a high-performing organization is further grounded.

A business case makes change management recognizable to business leaders

The business case format is familiar to senior organizational leaders and project leaders. The concepts and elements of planning, execution, objectives, scope, dependencies, milestones, and accountabilities are common to them and are used daily. In using a familiar format, people management is presented in a hard, logical manner that the solid-number-types of leaders are accustomed to working with.

Conclusion

No, there is no particular panacea for having a successful organization. There is no organizational culture that will guarantee success. The best that any organizational leader can hope to do is to take all of the resources available – including the tangible, the intangible, the objective, and the subjective – and attempt to put them together with the knowledge that he or she has that will bring the best results for the moment.

What you have been reading is nothing more than primer on some ideas, tools, the use of resources, and leadership techniques that have proven successful for many organizations. It is also a collection of experiences and lessons learned from this author's life in the business world and while walking and working alongside people in and from countless ethnic cultures and nations. Some things are universal. And one of those things is the respect that people want and desire from those around them.

As you concluded your reading, you may have come to the same epiphany that this author and many others have come to when charged with leading people.

True, lasting, meaningful personal success is not illustrated by how people perceive us or how they treat us. Rather true, personal success is defined by how we treat those around us. It is only when we have true, lasting, meaningful personal success that we can help others in their seeking success. There is a maxim, a proverb, a quote and a principle that sums up how to have the personal success that is true, lasing, and meaningful:

"We need to treat others as we would want them to treat us."

www.ingramcontent.com/pod-product-compliance
Lightning Source LLC
Chambersburg PA
CBHW041118210326
41518CB00031B/137